COMING TOGETHER IN CHRIST

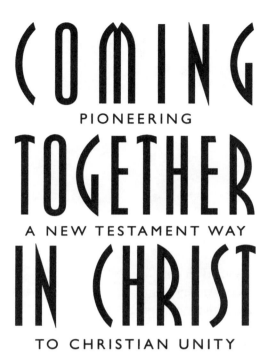

COMING

PIONEERING

TOGETHER

A NEW TESTAMENT WAY

IN CHRIST

TO CHRISTIAN UNITY

*CHRISTIAN CHURCHES / CHURCHES OF CHRIST
AND THE CHURCH OF GOD (ANDERSON)*

BARRY & JAMES
CALLEN NORTH

COLLEGE PRESS PUBLISHING COMPANY • JOPLIN, MISSOURI

Library of Congress Cataloging-in-Publication Data

Callen, Barry L.
    Coming together in Christ: pioneering a New Testament
way to Christian unity: Christian Churches/Churches of
Christ and the Church of God (Anderson) / Barry L. Callen,
James B. North.
       p.   cm.
    Includes bibliographical references and index.
    ISBN 0-89900-783-X (pbk.)
    1. Christian Churches and Churches of Christ—
Relations—Church of God (Anderson, Ind.) 2. Church
of God (Anderson, Ind.)—Relations—Christian Churches
and Churches of Christ. 3. Christian union. I. North,
James B. II. Title.
BX6799.C23C35 1997
280'.042—dc21   97-3137
                                                          CIP

TABLE OF CONTENTS

DEDICATION

In loving memory of Keith Huttenlocker,
a good brother in the faith and longtime leader in the
Church of God (Anderson), who contributed much to the
Open Forum dialogue, and in November, 1996, came
together fully with the saints of all ages and
the Christ whom he had served so well.

INTRODUCTION

Central to the message of the New Testament is the call for believers to come together in Christ. In fact, the little phrase *in Christ* is used frequently by St. Paul to identify what it means to be a Christian. It is Jesus Christ in whom we sinful humans find our redemption and in whom we also are made heirs of the riches of Christ (Eph. 1:7, 11). Once we have believed in Jesus as the Christ, we are "marked with the seal of the promised Holy Spirit" (Eph. 1:13). Christians, those truly in Christ, are then called to be caught up in God's larger purpose of bringing together "all things in him, things in heaven and things on earth" (Eph. 1:10). Paul emphasizes in Ephesians 1:11 the great coordinate truths of *in Christ* and *we*, the identity of the Christian in Christ and the intent of the resulting togetherness of believers in Christ.

Being in Christ is intended to bring about a unique and visible togetherness of all who are His. This divinely-enabled togetherness is the church, the new community brought into being by the received grace of Christ. The oneness of this body of Christ is to include the breaking down of the typical human divisions caused by ethnic, racial, economic, and gender barriers (Gal. 3:28). Sin of any kind is to divide no more. The Christ-origin and Christ-togetherness of the church community are intended to be a hopeful witness to a broken, divided, and despairing world.

This present book seeks to do several things. It traces the journey of two bodies of Christ's people who in recent years have sought to understand and implement more fully their similar historic burdens for being authentically Christian in Christ and meaningfully together in Christian unity for the sake of Christ's mission in our world. At one level, then, the book is historical. It informs the reader about these two particular bodies of Christians and the story of their recent quest to come closer together in Christ. It also provides select readings on Christian unity in the form of nine significant Appendices and traces across the twentieth century the search of the larger Christian community for a greater unity among believers worldwide (chapter one).

But this book's intent extends beyond mere history. A hope of the authors is that this work can both provide an important historical resource and be a prophetic voice to Christians who either do not yet sense the importance of being together in Christ or who are looking for practical ways to get on with the important task of implementing the unity God grants by grace, all for the sake of more effective Christian mission to a lost world.

What is Christ now saying to the church? In the midst of the recent process of the coming together in Christ that has been pursued by the Christian Churches/Churches of Christ and the Church of God (Anderson), what has been learned or done to date that is worthy of sharing? What of a mission nature has been accomplished to make all the effort worthwhile? Have these two bodies of Bible-believing Christians, each with its own distinctive tradition, found their way on the subject of Christian unity? Are they now better able to end their relative isolation and speak prophetically to Christians of different traditions (and to the many Christians in their own traditions who have not yet become involved)? Is there a way to overcome division among Christians without compromising the truth of the gospel itself? Is failing to search aggressively for such a way tolerable in the face of Christ's commission to evangelize the whole world?

The very writing process of this book has sought to model a coming together. The authors are widely recognized church historians, teachers, and writers in their respective church traditions. Barry Callen (Church of God) carried responsibility for the primary drafting of chapters one, four, and six. James North (Christian Churches/Churches of Christ) drafted chapters two, three, and five. They then critiqued each other's work and furthered the blending process of the writing so that the result would have coherence and consensus. Should the reader notice any differing styles of writing or slight duplication of material, the cause is the process of the writing. Such is the way of Christian unity, a real togetherness without any artificial and coerced sameness.

The quest for Christian unity for the sake of Christian mission was begun by Jesus himself (John 17:20-21). Now, burdened for generations that what Jesus began and for which he prayed must be fulfilled in our time, two groups of conservative Christians have sought ways that they themselves can more fully come together in Christ. Over recent years the involved theological and pastoral leaders have learned each other's histories, church cultures, and theological traditions, and have built appreciative and fruitful relationships. While not in the business of "compromise," lowest-common-denominator theology, or the merger-mentality kind of ecumenicity, they nonetheless have learned that each group is less than whole in the absence of the other. So they have persisted in their quest to get better acquainted and find ways to serve together.

The writers pray that this seeking may be only the beginning. May it inspire other believers to risk leaving the comfort zones of their denominational ghettos and join the journey to come together in Christ for the sake of the gospel witness to the world. We as Christians will be more the church that we ought to be and reach more effectively in mission as it ought to be *only* as we work at being together in Christ and are enabled for service by the power of the Spirit of Christ. One lesson is clearer now. We Christians need each other. Christian unity is both a gift and an achievement. The achievement is crucial for mission. If the church cannot get its own act together, how will the world ever believe? This book is about two groups of Christians who recognize God's gift of unity and have determined to work toward its more adequate achievement.

Appreciation is expressed to the D. & B. Bush Charitable Foundation for its generous support that helped make possible both this publication and the multi-year process of dialogue that it reports. Appreciation also is expressed for nineteenth-century prophetic pioneers like Alexander Campbell, Barton Stone, and Daniel Warner who had similar visions of God's will for the church. Theirs is a vision we are yet seeking to understand and fulfill as the twenty-first century fast approaches.

Barry Callen and James North
Anderson, Indiana, and Cincinnati, Ohio
April, 1997

Chapter One

SCENE: THE ECUMENICAL CENTURY

Why worry about the dividedness of God's people? Are not dozens of denominations and scores of conflicting creedal statements just the way it is and always has been? Is it not inevitable that disciples of Jesus will see some things differently and join what they prefer? Does any of this really matter all that much?

Maybe it really does matter. Maybe division is not inevitable. Maybe an easy apathy in the face of the fractured fellowship of God's children is actually an obstacle to the very purpose for which the church exists in a world of unbelievers. Maybe the divine intent is that there be a *united* church for a *divided* world.[1] This possibility is well worth our most careful attention.

When Did the Division Begin?

The visible brokenness of the Christian community roots back at least to the "Great Schism" (A.D. 1054) when

---

[1] This slogan, "a united church for a divided world," has been featured for many years on the national radio broadcast of the Church of God (Anderson). The broadcast, long known as the "Christian Brotherhood Hour," is now known by the new CBH words, "Christians Broadcasting Hope."

the Patriarch of Constantinople and the Pope of Rome
ended a long dispute by excommunicating each other. This
great split between the Eastern and Western churches,
reflecting differing cultural and theological tendencies,
was to persist for centuries. Adding to the magnitude of
this division, in the sixteenth century came the Protestant
Reformation with its break from the Roman Catholic
Church and the resulting proliferation of new denominational bodies that has gone on ever since. To be fair,
reformers like Martin Luther and John Calvin were seeking to correct, not fragment, even if fragmentation was the
result.

All of this division finally has been met in the twentieth century with widespread reconciling and peacemaking
attempts. The concern for Christian unity has moved to
the center of the church's agenda worldwide. For
Christians generally, the twentieth century often is
referred to as the "ecumenical" century. These have been
decades in which a major agenda item among the
churches worldwide has been the growing desire to somehow make meaningful and visible the intended oneness of
God's people. But there were earlier concerns and efforts
on behalf of Christian unity.

Quotations from the classic writings of major
Protestant reformers like John Calvin in the sixteenth
century[2] can be cited on behalf of a deep concern for the
wholeness of the church. In the eighteenth century, John
Wesley, for instance, was insistent that unity among
Christians constituted the very essence of the church and
that the mission of the church was hindered severely by
rampant division.[3]

The Stone-Campbell and Church of God (Anderson)
movements began in the nineteenth century. From their

---

[2]John Calvin, *Institutes of the Christian Religion*, trans. John Allen,
Vol. II, 7th ed. (Philadelphia: Presbyterian Board of Christian
Education, 1936), 271.

[3]See, e.g., Wesley's *Letter to a Roman Catholic* (1749) and *Catholic
Spirit* (1750).

beginnings they have carried a heavy burden for resolving the problem of Christian disunity. They, however, were isolated voices crying out on behalf of Christian unity in the midst of a nineteenth-century sectarian wilderness. Numerous and complex divisions among Christians have been all too typical in American religious history. In its wake has come "the sad spectacle of a seriously divided body of Christians and, too often, an unreasoning bigotry that was incapable of either the conversion of the sinners or the edification of the saints."[4]

Only in the twentieth century did the burden for the unity of Christian believers become shared widely. Often in recent decades this concern has surfaced in ways both strikingly similar to and significantly different from the earlier visions of prophetic voices like Alexander Campbell and Daniel Warner. The formalized ecumenical movement has emerged and operated largely outside the direct involvement and influence of these earlier unity movements (primarily by the conscious choice of these movements—an irony calling for careful explanation). Modern seekers after increased Christian unity, like Campbell and Warner before them, have looked to the Bible for guidance and inspiration.

Biblical and National Foundations

Both the ideal of Christian unity and the dilemma blocking its achievement appear to be rooted deeply in the American character. This nation is known as the United States, being both one and many, a united nation made up of fifty states. The ideal emerged in the Continental Congress of 1776 when the thirteen colonies joined against England by framing and signing the famous Declaration of Independence. The dilemma, however, had made this process of agreeing on the Declaration slow,

---

[4]Henry E. Webb, *In Search of Christian Unity: A History of the Restoration Movement* (Cincinnati: Standard Publishing, 1990), 378-379.

15

heated, and nearly impossible. The colonies had their differing cultures, economies, and commitments. They finally agreed to the necessary uniting for the common cause of freedom from foreign tyranny. But they soon insisted that, in any new togetherness, each be guaranteed significant freedom from the potential of tyranny from within the new whole. This was to be one nation, comprised of many semi-autonomous states.

Is the life of the church necessarily as political as this? Must there be a careful *division* of power so that there will be no *abuse* of power among Christ's disciples? Is Christianity inherently one reality or a collection of separate realities joined by something which holds all the diversity in a delicate unity? How are Christians to live out the central affirmation that there is "one hope, one faith, one baptism, and one God" (Eph. 4:4-6)? In what sense, if any, should there be one church in the midst of all our human differences, even inside the community of faith? Where does all this division come from?

Does the dividedness among Christian people arise primarily from sincere differences in perception about what Christians should believe and practice? Often it does, but not always. In his classic 1929 study *The Social Sources of Denominationalism*,[5] author H. Richard Niebuhr argued disturbingly that the distinctive denominational character of American Christianity was rooted primarily in the social divisions of class, race, and region of the country. A significant factor separating Baptists and Methodists, for example, was their difference in social status in the society. Protestants and Catholics were in tension largely because of their different immigration histories and resettlement patterns. The very humanness of Christian people apparently is one key factor leading to their dividedness.

While lamentable, it is true that divisions among Christians are as old as the faith itself. The problem of Christian disunity was first evidenced in the New

---

[5]H. Richard Niebuhr, *The Social Sources of Denominationalism* (New York: World, 1929).

Testament. Following Jesus' resurrection from the dead, the new faith in our victorious Lord had to accomplish at least two things. First, it had to understand itself in relation to the Jewish heritage from which it came and in the midst of which it first flourished. There was continuity with the "Old" and also discontinuity since the "New" had come. Within only a few decades after the resurrection of the Jewish Messiah, Jesus, many of his Jewish followers were leading a vigorous move to separate themselves from identity with the nonbelieving Jewish community. Division in the community of faith was soon a reality.

Second, the new faith had to express the meaning of its believing in various cultural settings far beyond its Hebrew roots. This theological task, acted out on the earliest mission fields, labored to communicate the faith in Greek and Roman settings. The early Christian evangelists and church planters sought creatively to cross language and cultural barriers for the sake of effective proclamation to all the world. Soon there was introduced into the young church a variety of theological expressions and organizational patterns, all claiming in their separate places to be appropriate applications of the one gospel of Jesus Christ. Thus, there was inevitable diversity.

Does such a variety of expressions and applications of the faith mean increasing *division* in the church or merely an inevitable and acceptable pluralism of the church on mission? Must there be a singularity of creedal and organizational form among Christians for there to be the unity that Jesus expects and the Holy Spirit intends to enable? Is there one right way of saying things and doing things so that any deviation is an intolerable act of disunity? Or is it the case that the conference on Faith and Order held in Edinburgh, Scotland in 1937 was right when it announced that what it desired was "the unity of a living organism, with the diversity characteristic of the members of a healthy body"?[6]

---

[6]Cited in *A Documentary History of the Faith and Order Movement*, ed. Lukas Vischer (St. Louis: Bethany Press, 1963), 63. In the New Delhi,

17

There are several keynotes of the biblical revelation that are basic to the vision of Christian unity. They all are based first in the affirmed oneness of God. The unity of humankind with God was broken by the one man, Adam, and now has been restored by the one man, Jesus Christ (1 Cor. 15:22). This restored relationship with God in Christ is to be evident in the people who accept their reconciliation by faith and are called to express their reconciliation through participation in the church. Being one in Christ, they are to be one in Christ's body, the church. Believers are to share their oneness with God through communion with God and God's people. Within the church there are many gifts and ministries which together, in their rich diversity and essential interdependence, make up the unity of the church (1 Cor. 12:4-30). Divisive factors that rupture relationships in this body are sinful and damaging to the effectiveness of church mission. They are foreign to the biblical vision of the church as a new reality in Christ.

The triune God intends that we human beings be gathered into a corporate, reconciling whole, a special divine-human community which

> . . . not only reflects God's own eternal reality but actually participates in that reality. Since the New Testament era the focal point of the reconciled society in history has been the church of Jesus Christ. . . . As that people, we are called to pioneer in the present the community of love and thereby to participate in and reflect the eternal relation of the triune God. . . .[7]

The New Testament rebukes the mentalities and practices that later would help produce numerous and destructive divisions in the church. These include:

India, Assembly of the World Council of Churches (1961) there was the clear statement that "unity does not imply simple uniformity of organization, rite or expression" (Ibid., 145).

[7]Stanley J. Grenz, *Revisioning Evangelical Theology* (Downers Grove, IL: InterVarsity Press, 1993), 188.

1. *Autonomy/Factionalism*—I will pick the church leaders worthy of respect and help form partisan groups to advance the programs and views I prefer (1 Cor. 1:10-17; 3:1-23);
2. *Lust for Power*—It is important that I be in charge in the church (Matt. 20:20-28; Acts 8:9-24; Phil. 2:1-11; 1 Peter 5:1-3; 3 John 9);
3. *Unwillingness to Seek Reconciliation*—I am right and am satisfied to see other believers separated from me (Matt. 5:23-26; 18:15-20; Rom. 12:18; Eph. 4:3; Phil. 2:1-4; 1 Thess. 5:13; Heb. 12:14; James 3:17);
4. *Failure to Maintain Church Discipline*—I will let things be however they are, good or bad (Matt. 18:15-20; 1 Cor. 5);
5. *Inattention to Doctrinal and Practical Purity*—Toleration is a primary virtue; it keeps peace among disagreeing believers (1 Tim. 4; 6:11-21; 2 Tim. 1:13f; 2:14–4:5; Titus; etc.); and
6. *Failure to Help Fellow Believers in Need*—I will enjoy what God has given me and be comfortable in allowing others to live with whatever God has or has not given them (Matt. 25:31-46; 3 John).

In the face of such attitudes, all too frequent in church life, Christians remain faced with the prayer of Jesus. Just as he and his Father are one, Jesus prayed earnestly that all his disciples should likewise be one (John 17). The modern movement on behalf of Christian unity has taken this prayer seriously and has sought in various ways to do something about it. Why? The primary reason, as Jesus said, is "that the world may believe that God has sent me" (John 17:21).

The bylaws of the Faith and Order Commission of the World Council of Churches state this body's purpose in a way intended to reflect directly this prayer of Jesus. The Commission's purpose is "to proclaim the oneness of the church of Jesus Christ and to call the churches to the goal of visible unity in one faith, and one eucharistic fellowship expressed in worship and in common life in Christ in order that the world may believe." An underlying assumption is that the credibility of the proclamation of good news in Jesus Christ is dependent in large part on the impression conveyed to people generally by the witnessing community of Christians. Are Christians a reconciling community and are they themselves an obviously reconciled community of faith? The classic biblical statement of God's intent for the church is the Ephesian letter, especially verses 4:4-6 where we are told that there is only one body, one faith, and one baptism, and that believers should make every effort to keep it that way, relying on the work of the Spirit and the bonding power of peace and love.

The "Ecumenical" Movement

Why call these recent coming-together efforts "ecumenical"? The original Greek word *oikoumene* meant "the inhabited world." From this concept of the whole world, it was a short step to the early Christian practice of convening ecumenical councils, that is, councils of Christian leaders from all over the world. In the twentieth century the concept has been broadened to include the gathering of leaders from all segments of the Christian community (multidenominational and multinational). Thus, "ecumenical" has come to mean the move to somehow unite Christians who are separated from each other by differing creeds, structures, and traditions. It refers to the modern Christian effort to establish meaningful unity in teaching, practice, and mission among all the Christian communities of "the inhabited earth." It roots in the concern for Christians to realize the intended unity of the church and the eventual unity of all things in Jesus Christ.

Already in nineteenth-century America prophetic voices were crying out against the numerous and often acrimonious divisions in Christ's body, the church. For example, in 1809 Thomas Campbell issued his *Declaration and Address* in which he boldly announced that "division among Christians is a horrid evil." He insisted that the "bitter jarrings and janglings of a party spirit" so commonly evidenced among the denominations had to be overcome.[8] Much later in the century Daniel Warner carried a similar burden. God surely does not passively permit rampant division among believers. To the contrary, Warner insisted, the dividedness among Christian people is not just unfortunate; it is inappropriate and wholly unacceptable. Unity is clearly God's will for the church.[9] Church unity should be celebrated as a divine gift. The gift is realized best when there is a common embracing of the simple gospel as described in the New Testament and is still available through the enlightenment and power of the Holy Spirit.

Did not Jesus make it plain? His disciples are supposed to be one so that the world may know (John 17). Mission and unity are interdependent. Accordingly, it was the modern mission enterprise of the church ("that the world may know") that precipitated the significant concern of the twentieth century for a renewed oneness of the church. Rampant denominationalism might make some sense in Ohio or Oklahoma, but it had become obvious that it was a hindrance when missionaries tried to transplant this complex of division to cultures completely unacquainted with the good news of Jesus Christ. Surely the main concern of missionaries should be to make disciples for Jesus, not necessarily to make more converts for the Anglicans, Presbyterians, Baptists, or Methodists. The growth of the missionary movement led the sending churches to see more clearly the scandal of their often competing efforts to preach the gospel in distant lands.

There always have been those believers burdened for the unity of the church. It was, however, the extensive missionary movement of the nineteenth century that laid

---

[8]Thomas Campbell, *Declaration and Address*, 24, 47.

[9]See the biography of Daniel Warner by Barry L. Callen, *It's God's Church! Life and Legacy of Daniel Sidney Warner* (Anderson, IN: Warner Press, 1995).

the immediate groundwork for the ecumenical focus of the twentieth century. This focus first came dramatically into view in Scotland. In 1910 there was convened in Edinburgh an interdenominational missionary conference. This great gathering brought together for ten days of serious discussion about 1,300 delegates representing 160 missionary boards and societies. The discussion was organized around eight topics, including the conveying of the gospel to all the non-Christian world and how better to cooperate and promote greater unity in this grand enterprise. Out of this conference came a permanent representative body, the International Missionary Council formed in 1921. Its main roles were to coordinate increased missionary cooperation worldwide and to speak with a single voice to governments concerning the missionary work of multiple bodies in their lands.

The Edinburgh World Missionary Conference and its aftermaths are seen generally as the launching of the modern ecumenical movement. Soon to come were the devastating effects, especially in Europe, of two world wars and the discrediting by Karl Barth and "neo-orthodoxy" of the "liberal" theologies so influential since the nineteenth century. Following World War II, various strands of the ongoing ecumenical experimentations finally were merged in 1948 (Amsterdam, Holland) to form the World Council of Churches. At its launching, the WCC was comprised of 145 church bodies from 44 countries. These numbers have grown to 300 Protestant, Anglican, and Orthodox churches from 100 countries. The Roman Catholic Church now participates at least in the WCC's Commission on Faith and Order. At its New Delhi Assembly (1961), the WCC identified itself as "a fellowship of churches which confess the Lord Jesus Christ as God and Saviour according to the scriptures and therefore seek to fulfill their common calling to the glory of the one God, Father, Son and Holy Spirit." The Trinitarian emphasis of this statement reflected in part the strong theological view of the Orthodox churches.

The World Council of Churches is not the whole of the ecumenical movement by any means; it is, however, its most widely recognized formalization worldwide. The whole would include the lessening within Roman Catholicism of its traditional exclusiveness. Rome's Vatican Council II in the 1960s brought a new openness that included an altered Roman Catholic view of those many non-Roman Christians. "Heretics" now were elevated in Rome's eyes to "separated brethren." In 1965 Pope Paul and the Orthodox Patriarch of Constantinople issued joint nullifications of the excommunications of each other, a dramatic division that had stood since 1054!

Similar efforts at renewed Christian unity were occurring in the United States across the twentieth century. In 1895 a group of ministers in New York City organized the Federation of Churches and Christian Workers, an experiment that led in 1908 to the creation on a larger scale of the Federal Council of the Churches of Christ in America. Thirty denominations were charter members. The preamble to the FCC's constitution was the only assumption of doctrinal commitment expected of all participants. The FCC said it was "to manifest the essential oneness of the Christian churches of America in Jesus Christ as their divine Lord and Savior." This Council announced respect for the autonomy of its member denominations and soon reflected a strong concern for a united influencing of select social issues, publishing in 1912 the "Social Creed of the Churches." Some members, and especially conservative leaders from non-participating churches, became critical of various public stances and actions of the Council.

In 1948 the FCC used its experience and leadership in interdenominational relations to encourage the founding of the World Council of Churches. The work of the FCC and a series of parallel efforts in the United States finally were combined in 1950 to form the National Council of Churches. Ever since, this NCC and the National Association of Evangelicals (see below) have been the primary vehicles in the United States for seeking to express a united American Protestantism. The need was obvious. Following World War II the religious landscape of America was shaped by the divisions between Protestants and Catholics, Christians and Jews, and members of different Protestant denominations of Christians. Suspicions of other faith communities "lurked very near the surface and sometimes erupted in vitriolic denouncements."[10]

In neighboring Canada there emerged one of the more comprehensive examples of approaching increased Christian unity by the merger of churches into a single organization. In 1925 the Methodist Church of Canada, Congregational Union of Canada, much of the Presbyterian Church in Canada, and the Council of Local Union Churches merged to form the United Church of Canada. The resulting denomination was "the first modern church in the world fully to unite such diverse traditions in one religious body."[11] Joining later were the Wesleyan Methodist Church of Bermuda (1930) and the Canada Conference of the Evangelical United Brethren (1968).

One conclusion of all the experimentation on behalf of Christian unity by the World Council of Churches has been a clarification of the Council's primary purpose. This purpose is "to call the churches to the goal of visible unity in one faith and in one eucharistic fellowship" (Constitution of WCC, III, 1). Three essential conditions or elements of visible unity now have been identified: (1) the common confession of the apostolic faith; (2) the mutual recognition of baptism, eucharist and ministry; and (3) common structures for witness and service as well as for decision-making and teaching authoritatively.[12]

---

[10]Robert Wuthnow, *The Restructuring of American Religion* (Princeton, NJ: Princeton University Press, 1988), 79.

[11]Daniel Reid, coordinating editor, *Dictionary of Christianity in America* (Downers Grove, IL: InterVarsity Press, 1990), 1198.

[12]*Confessing the One Faith: An Ecumenical Explication of the Apostolic Faith as it is Confessed in the Nicene-Constantinopolitan Creed (381)*, Faith and Order Paper No. 153 (Geneva, Switz.: WCC Publications, 1991), 1. The earlier Lima text on *Baptism, Eucharist and Ministry* is

These essential conditions for visible unity are based on several theological affirmations put forward clearly by Michael Kinnamon, an active ecumenical participant representing the Disciples of Christ denomination. In brief, they are:

1. The sovereignty of God "relativizes *all* human concepts, institutions, and activities";

2. The foundation of all Christian identity is "the biblical confession of Jesus as Christ and Lord (Matt. 16:16)";

3. In spite of the caution of point one, there is ultimate truth about God. It is revealed "in Christ" and is accessible to human beings "through the witness of Scripture";

4. The ultimate truth available in Christ and known through Scripture is "less propositional than 'personal,'" so that Jesus Christ, as opposed, for instance, to theories about him, is "the way, and the truth, and the life" (John 14:6). Those who wish to know truth "are invited into living relationship with him."

5. The church and its intended unity is crucial in part because "the diverse community of fellow Christians is an essential component of, and context for, the search for truth. Realizing that our interpretations of God's truth are partial . . . we also realize that we need each other if we are serious about being the church God wills."[13]

It has become an axiom of the ecumenical movement that *unity* does not imply *uniformity*. A certain diversity will remain inevitable—and can be a crucial enrichment contributing to the health of the whole. Hans Küng says that "pluralism can be a source of freedom and creativity in the Church. The diamond of Christian truth has many facets; difference is not bad, only difference hardened into

---

seen as a major addressing of the second of these essential conditions of visible unity (Faith and Order Paper No. 111, WCC, Geneva, 1982).

[13]Michael Kinnamon, *Truth and Community: Diversity and Its Limits in the Ecumenical Movement* (Grand Rapids: Eerdmans, 1988), 19-28.

exclusiveness."[14] Reported one prominent ecumenical leader, the goal is to draw . . .

> our attention away from our divisions directing us to that giving and receiving life and love which flow between the persons of the Holy Trinity. This mysterious life of divine communion is one in which the personal and relational are prior; in which multiplicity is perfectly held together so that there is no separation, while at the same time the very unity is enriched by the multiplicity, so that it never degenerates into arid uniformity.[15]

Exclusiveness, however, has hardly been the problem among the "mainline" denominations in recent decades. As leaders in the ecumenical movement, prominent mainline denominations (Disciples of Christ, Presbyterian Church [U.S.A.], United Methodist Church, etc.) have lost numbers, dollars, and constituent loyalty. There has been a weakening of the role of interdenominational agencies that have relied for their support on cooperating denominational systems such as these.

Lyle Schaller lists twenty-seven events and trends that, especially since the 1970s, have undermined the influence, authority, internal loyalty, and institutional strength of a series of these large Protestant denominations.[16] One result has been that the key players in cooperative church life have shifted from denominations and denominational officials to pastors and congregational leaders. Younger pastors now often complain that their denominations have moved from existing primarily to resource congregations to being too-aloof and too-expensive regulatory agencies.

---

[14]Hans Küng, *Reforming the Church Today* (New York: Crossroad Publishing, 1990), 32.

[15]Mary Tanner, "The Tasks of the World Conference in the Perspective of the Future" in Thomas Best and Günther Gassmann, eds., *On the Way to Fuller Koinonia* (Geneva, Switz.: World Council Publications, 1994), 24.

[16]Lyle Schaller, *21 Bridges to the 21st Century* (Nashville: Abingdon Press, 1994), 133-135.

These pastors do more than complain—they have created and joined extra-denominational networks of many kinds. Are denominations becoming "cultural dinosaurs"?

Reaction From the Right

"Conservative" Christians typically have been suspicious of the real intent and commitments of the World Council of Churches (and the National Council in the United States). They have refused to be identified with them and have been consistently critical. There has developed new division over how best to unify!

The vision of the modern ecumenical movement apparently involves a necessary tension between definitive Christian truth and diverse communities of Christian people. The central question facing the ecumenical movement may be "how to determine the limits of acceptable diversity."[17] Evangelicals have feared that numerous leaders committed to "ecumenicity" are more committed to achieving a visible unity of the churches than they are to maintaining biblically-based truth claims judged by many believers to be essential for any acceptable unity.

Many conservative Christian leaders choose to weigh very heavily their concern for the centrality of the "truth" as they understand it to be biblically revealed. J. Kenneth Grider, for example, worries about a "monolithic denomination" and observes that in Christian history "revival times have often occasioned a new order in Roman Catholicism or a new denomination in Protestantism—not mergers." His central concern is that "a wide-scoped merger of denominations could result in scarcely more than a mutually agreed upon near-vacuity of belief."[18] This concern has tended to characterize the many church bodies that have stayed outside the formal ecumenical movement. Even when recalling the classic statement of

---

[17]Kinnamon, *Truth and Community*, vii.

[18]J. Kenneth Grider, *A Wesleyan-Holiness Theology* (Kansas City: Beacon Hill Press, 1994), 484-485.

Willem Visser 't Hooft, first general secretary of the World Council of Churches, most evangelicals tend to distrust it. He declared in 1966 that, if the widespread interest in "pluralism" leads to relativism, one truth perspective judged to be as good as another, then he was opposed to pluralism as an invention of the devil.[19]

Many agree, but assume that prominent councils of churches do not. Suspicion and stereotyping exist on every hand. There is the supposed hurtful tendency of ecumenists "to dismiss evangelicalism as interested only in its version of truth at the expense of unity," while evangelicals often dismiss ecumenism "as interested only in its vision of unity at the expense of truth."[20]

In the wake of the formation of the World Council of Churches in 1948, an International Convention of Evangelicals was convened in the Netherlands in 1951. There the World Evangelical Fellowship was formed, in large part to provide the structure and forum for evangelicals worldwide to join in defending the faith and spreading the gospel to all the world.

Billy Graham spoke for many "conservative" Christians when he keynoted the great gathering of mission-minded mission leaders in Lausanne, Switzerland, in 1974. He reported that something negative had happened after the Edinburgh Conference of 1910. "It was," he said, "only a small cloud on the horizon, but it became a cyclone that swept the world." The core of Graham's concern was that early in the twentieth century "theological changes were subtly infiltrating Christian youth movements, causing some to weaken their ties to orthodox faith. The authority of evangelism began to shift from the Scriptures to the organized church. They focused attention on the materialistic salvation of the *community* rather than the individual. This became known as the 'Social Gospel.' Emphasis

---

[19]Willem Visser 't Hooft, "Pluralism—Temptation or Opportunity?" *Ecumenical Review*, April, 1966, 147.

[20]Kinnamon, *Truth and Community*, 14.

turned to man 'in this world,' rather than 'in this *and* the next world.'"[21]

In similar fashion, church historian James North has written about the Stone-Campbell or Restorationist Movement that crossed most of the nineteenth century, but was nearly destroyed early in the twentieth by many in this tradition accepting "religious liberalism."[22] It seems that those who embrace "liberalism," the Disciples of Christ in this case, also tend to become leaders in ecumenical efforts. Are openness, tolerance, and visible togetherness to be considered the primary Christian virtues?

By contrast, Billy Graham intended the Lausanne Congress of 1974 to convene "as one body, obeying one Lord, facing one world, with one task."[23] In listing his personal hopes for this Congress, he included: "I hope that a new 'koinonia' or fellowship among evangelicals of all persuasions will be developed throughout the world." He announced his belief that the Lord was saying to the church, "Let's go forward together in a worldwide fellowship in evangelism, in missions, in Bible translation, in literature distribution, in meeting world social needs, in evangelical theological training, etc."[24]

Graham pictured a derailed ecumenical movement. Initially in this century the movement had been fired by missionary zeal that was rooted in strong biblical convictions about human sin and salvation. But from Edinburgh, he said, there emerged two major streams of the modern missionary movement. He called the one "evangelical" and the other "ecumenical." We already have

---

[21]J.D. Douglas, ed., *Let the Earth Hear His Voice: International Congress on World Evangelization, Lausanne, Switzerland* (Minneapolis: World Wide Publications, 1975), 26.

[22]James North, *Union In Truth: An Interpretive History of the Restoration Movement* (Cincinnati: Standard Publishing, 1994), chapter ten.

[23]Ibid., 27.

[24]Ibid., 34.

reviewed what Graham saw as the ecumenical. What about the evangelical stream?

The evangelical stream of the modern missionary movement—and evangelicalism generally—has focused on evangelism based on clear "truth" more than on the concern for Christian unity as such. To put it more strongly, evangelicalism has reacted quite negatively to what appears to it as contrived structural attempts at unity, with negotiated theological compromises as centerpieces of the effort to be visibly united. A prime example was an effort that first surfaced in 1960 as a suggested merger of several mainline denominations.

Known popularly as "COCU" (Consultation on Church Union), by 1966 there had emerged from its cooperative explorations the document *Principles of Church Union* that reflected considerable consensus among its participating mainline denominations. Then in 1970 came *A Plan of Union for the Church of Christ Uniting*, but it was judged by many involved to be too bureaucratic. At its seventeenth plenary in 1988, COCU called on its churches to affirm "covenanting" as a means of visible union. Failing to date to accomplish a major structural solution to disunity, COCU has turned to exploring avenues to unity other than a merger of existing church organizations.[25]

Neither the Independent Christian Churches/Churches of Christ nor the Church of God (Anderson) has demonstrated any desire to be identified formally with either the WCC, the NCC, or COCU.[26] In general, they have chosen

---

[25]For a brief overview of the history of COCU, see Keith Watkins, "Twenty Years with the Consultation on Church Union," *Mid-Stream* 34:3 (July/October, 1995), 93-103.

[26]This is not to say that prominent individual leaders have not participated at least as interested and appreciative observers. At least the Church of God has seen some of its national agencies participate actively in select program units of the NCC, although not formally in the Council itself. Since 1984 Gilbert Stafford has represented the Commission on Christian Unity of the Church of God at North American meetings of Faith and Order. For his reflections on this, see Appendix H.

to remain aloof from the formalized ecumenical movement because they have judged it the wrong way to answer the right question. To be fair, the councils insist that they neither have nor desire any "superchurch" characteristics. They claim not to seek any enforced conformity or contrived church mergers, not to seek the advancement of any specific theology of the church or particular plan for the church's unity. They are, in their own view, merely fellowships of churches that enable increased Christian cooperation in the advancing of the cause of Christ.

Nonetheless, the National Council in the United States, for instance, has been resisted by many "conservative" bodies for one or more of the following reasons:

(1) The Council steadfastly refused to adopt as a basis of fellowship the hard core of generally accepted Biblical Christian doctrine; (2) It admitted into its membership a host of liberals who denied these doctrines and gave them preferred status in Council leadership; (3) It had created an ecclesiastical oligarchy which might easily develop into a superchurch; (4) Non-Council churches were forced to take protective measures to insure unfettered liberty in preaching the gospel; (5) It refused to state its acceptance of the Bible as the authoritative Word of God; (6) It considered man's need and not God's grace as motivation for social action, and the amelioration of the social order as of greater concern than the salvation of souls; (7) It seriously threatened a distinctly evangelistic thrust in foreign missionary work; (8) It encouraged social revolution to displace capitalism and condoned communism; (9) Its relations with the Eastern Orthodox Catholic churches and its general attitude toward Roman Catholicism threatened to weaken its Protestant testimony; (10) It deliberately omitted to include provisions for the preservation and perpetuation of all the values and liberties inherent in Protestantism.[27]

---

[27]James D. Murch, *Christians Only: A History of the Restoration Movement* (Cincinnati: Standard Publishing, 1962), 349.

31

Given such a critique, what is the alternative? Some
Christian individuals and churches standing outside the
World and National Councils began some efforts of their
own. More than criticism was called for. Needed was an
increased championing of common commitments to what
biblically-oriented believers understood should transcend
denominational divisions. Increasingly it has become clear
that "evangelicals" sense more affinity with each other
than with members of their own denominations who challenge and deny central aspects of what for centuries has
been "orthodox" Christian belief. By at least the 1960s the
time had come for concerted action designed to increase
some meaningful expression of Christian unity for the
sake of Christian mission.

Time for Evangelicals To Mature

In 1941 Carl McIntire led in forming the American
Council of Churches, demanding strict separation from the
Federal Council and the liberal theology it was said to represent. The following year in Chicago other conservatives,
less reactionary and separatist, launched the National
Association of Evangelicals. This body would grow to some
10 million members. It featured a "conservative" creedal
statement based on the belief that the Bible is "the only
infallible, authoritative, Word of God." The social agenda of
the NAE certainly differed from that of the Federal
Council (and later the National Council) and it made clear
that it had no aspirations to being a "superchurch." Soon
its efforts were helped greatly by the founding in 1956 of
the significant magazine, *Christianity Today*.

More recently there have been a few developments that
indicate a maturing among evangelicals in regard to their
concern for Christian unity, whatever the shortcomings of
the ecumenical movement in general. One was the "World
Congress on Evangelism" that convened in Berlin in 1966.
It was the dream of evangelist Billy Graham and featured
as its theme "One Race, One Gospel, One Task."

Participants from over 100 nations concurred gladly in the closing statement of the Congress, which read in part:

> As an evangelical ecumenical gathering of Christian disciples and workers, we cordially invite all believers in Christ to unite in the common task of bringing the word of salvation to mankind in spiritual revolt and moral chaos. . . . Recognizing that the ministry of reconciliation is given to us all, we seek to enlist every believer and to close the ranks of all Christians for an effective witness to our world.[28]

Another prominent example of intentional action occurred in July, 1974, when some 4,000 Christians representing 151 countries gathered in Lausanne, Switzerland, to participate in the "International Congress on World Evangelization." The central concern of this event, called together by the Billy Graham Evangelistic Association, was to stimulate the designing and implementation of strategies to complete the task of the Great Commission of Jesus. The resulting "Lausanne Covenant," agreed to by nearly all participants, reads in part: "Thus a growing partnership of churches will develop and the universal character of Christ's Church will be more clearly exhibited."[29] This Covenant, in discussing the central task of world evangelization, likewise recognized: "Evangelism summons us to unity, because our oneness strengthens our witness, just as our disunity undermines our gospel reconciliation."

Then in 1977 a group of forty-six evangelical leaders met in a suburb of Chicago. They expressed gratitude for the evangelical resurgence being experienced in the country at the time, but charged that "evangelicals are hindered from achieving full maturity by a reduction of the historic faith." One element of this reduction that was addressed in their final "Chicago Call: An Appeal to Evangelicals" had to do with Christian unity. They said in part:

---

[28]Carl F.H. Henry and W. Stanley Mooneyham, eds., *One Race, One Gospel, One Task* (Minneapolis: World Wide Publications, 1967), I:5-6.

[29]J.D. Douglas, ed., *Let the Earth Hear His Voice*, 6.

We deplore the scandalous isolation and separation of Christians from one another. We believe such division is contrary to Christ's explicit desire for unity among his people and impedes the witness of the church in the world. Evangelicalism is too frequently characterized by an ahistorical, sectarian mentality. We fail to appropriate the catholicity of historic Christianity, as well as the breadth of the biblical revelation.

Of course, these evangelical leaders were not promoting church union at any cost; but they were being critical of the common tendency to spiritualize concepts of church unity and thereby enable many Christians to default in good conscience on the responsibility to make such unity real and visible. Where should Christians begin? These leaders called on evangelicals to "humbly and critically scrutinize our respective traditions, renounce sacred shibboleths, and recognize that God works within diverse historical streams." This recognition does not necessarily lead to "doctrinal indifferentism," they insisted.[30]

What it does lead to is a healthy humility. As Christian Churches' scholar Frederick Norris insists: "We must recognize our oneness in the midst of our diversity. . . . Surely we can begin to understand, both because of the New Testament and patristic evidence, and our own sense of the relativity of cultures and individual experiences, that the one true Church is illusive and not represented in its fullness by any one tradition." He adds: "Whether as Roman Catholics or Evangelical Protestants, we belong to the more basic community of those who seek to be catholic Christians."[31] Others have called for believers to be "evangelical-catholics."[32]

---

[30]"The Chicago Call," as quoted in *Christianity Today*, June 17, 1977, 28-29.

[31]Frederick Norris, *The Apostolic Faith: Protestants and Roman Catholics* (Collegeville, MN: The Liturgical Press, 1992), 117, xv.

[32]Clark Pinnock and Robert Brow, *Unbounded Love: A Good News Theology for the 21st Century* (Downers Grove, IL: InterVarsity Press, 1994), 137.

A concern for catholicity (wholeness of the universal church) lies deep in the Christian tradition. To be "catholic" in this context means to claim the rich heritage all believers have in the larger Christian tradition that stretches across twenty centuries. Both Norris and Barry Callen of the Church of God (Anderson) tradition use the phrase "free-church catholic" as a positive description of the ideal in view.[33] James Earl Massey of the Church of God (Anderson) emphasizes that denominated Christian bodies can be honorable and effective, but only if they are not honored as ends in themselves. They are to function cooperatively in relation to the whole body for the sake of the health and effectiveness of the whole body of believers. He says:

> No one form should be judged divisive just because it is a form. . . . Diversity is not division when the spirit of relating to those beyond the group is kept alive. . . . Diversity is one thing, while a *spirit* of division is quite another. . . . Every Christian has a legacy in every other Christian. We experience that legacy only as we receive each other and relate, moving eagerly beyond group boundaries.[34]

F. Burton Nelson has called for an increased maturation of evangelicalism in relation to the pressing issue of the unity of God's church. Such maturing, he admits, will mean at least:

> ...humbly supporting the belief that evangelicals need the whole church in their pilgrimage toward maturation, and at the same time unashamedly maintaining that the whole church needs the evangelical witness in order for there to be a balanced perspective.

> ...resisting the false dichotomy between *evangelical* on the one hand and *ecumenical* on the other, insisting

---

[33]Norris, *The Apostolic Faith*, xxvii, and Callen, *Contours of a Cause: The Theological Vision of the Church of God Movement* (Anderson University School of Theology, 1995), 41.

[34]James Earl Massey, *Concerning Christian Unity* (Anderson, IN: Warner Press, 1979), 75, 78, 82.

rather that it is possible to be both passionately evangelical and, simultaneously, passionately ecumenical.[35]

The twentieth century, often called the ecumenical century, also has seen the dramatic rise and considerable impact of the "pentecostal" or "charismatic" movement. While it is true that the traditional focus of this movement on particular gifts of the Spirit often has been divisive, it also is true that renewed focus on vibrant life in the Spirit has crossed denominational lines and been a unifying force among millions of Christians.

The same can be said of gospel music and a recent movement among Christian men. The annual "Praise Gathering" of Bill and Gloria Gaither in Indianapolis, for instance, surely is a significant "ecumenical" event among sincere evangelical Christians who come to rejoice in the gospel without regard to their various denominational identifications. The 1990 founding and subsequent success of "Promise Keepers" has highlighted for tens of thousands of participants the identity and responsibilities of Christian men, with an obvious and wholesome disregard for the men's many denominational affiliations.[36]

Joining gospel music and this Christian men's movement as unifying forces has been the widely understood responsibility of Christians to be effective bearers of the good news in Christ. Evangelicals, while cautious about the formalized ecumenical movement, have become aggressive about forming networks centered around the accomplishment of the church's evangelistic mission. A good example is the 1991 formation of "Churches Uniting in Global Mission" (CUGM). Note five apparent differences between this more recent uniting effort and that of the Consultation on Church Union (COCU) that was launched in 1962:

---

[35]Nelson, in Robert Webber and Donald Bloesch, eds., *The Orthodox Evangelicals* (Nashville: Thomas Nelson, 1978), 208.
[36]See a major story on "Promise Keepers" in *Christianity Today* (February 6, 1995).

1. COCU was created to advance institutional mergers. CUGM was created to advance mission, witness, and outreach.
2. The leadership of COCU is vested largely in denominational structures and denominational officers. The leadership of CUGM is vested in senior ministers.
3. COCU brings together people from a relatively narrow band of Protestant traditions. CUGM brings leaders together from a huge array of traditions from liberal to fundamentalist.
4. After many years of frustration in promoting organic union, COCU has moved cooperation in ministry to the top of the agenda. Within weeks of its official birth, CUGM had delivered tons of food to hungry people in Russia.
5. COCU works with and through denominational structures. CUGM works with and through individuals, congregations, and ad hoc groups.[37]

Movements like the Independent Christian Churches and the Church of God (Anderson) have tended to remain ecumenically uninvolved, even from conservative associations like the NAE. These two church movements, both caring deeply about Christian unity, are not organizational "joiners" by tradition (they have seen too much human organizing in church life become instruments of more Christian disunity). They have tended to see "fundamentalistic" characteristics and too heavy a Calvinistic theological emphasis in the NAE. In addition, the NAE's creedal basis for membership has seemed to them only a furtherance of the traditional Protestant condoning of denominationalism as inevitable and thus acceptable.[38] After all, the Church of God movement, for instance, began in part because an earlier cooperative church organization, the National Holiness Association, took a similar

---

[37]Schaller, *21 Bridges*, 137.

[38]See James G. Van Buren, "Views and Reviews," *Christian Standard*, October 6, 1951, 14-15. Individual members of the Christian Churches and the Church of God, however, sometimes have participated, even assumed leadership roles.

stance of expecting standard denominational credentials of its members.[39]

The Burnley Lane Beginning

The twentieth century has been characterized by a heightened concern for a renewed unity among Christians. Numerous unifying efforts have worked in various directions, arising sometimes from differing visions of the goal. As the century now closes, the following observation represents well much of the current circumstance:

> The true church is found wherever the gospel is truly preached and truly received. Denominational allegiance is clearly of less than ultimate significance; the criterion of being saved has nothing to do with which church or fellowship one attends, but with whether one has heard and responded to the gospel. In an age in which social mobility has emerged as a major cultural force, evangelical ecclesiology has proved to be a winner.[40]

There appear to be two equally important challenges, parallel challenges often difficult to address equally and simultaneously. They are "both to pursue relationships of oneness, peace, and reconciliation and to be faithful to the God of truth. Focusing on the first without being equally concerned with the second may lead to a tepid relatedness; focusing on the second without being equally concerned with the first may lead to a smug separateness."[41] Similarly, church historian James North identifies the two central foci of the Restoration Movement as the concern for Christian union and for biblical authority. Thomas Campbell used the phrase "Union in Truth" in his famous

---

[39]See Barry Callen, *It's God's Church!*

[40]Alister McGrath, "Why Evangelicalism is the Future of Protestantism," in *Christianity Today* (June 19, 1995), 23.

[41]Gilbert Stafford, *Theology for Disciples* (Anderson, IN: Warner Press, 1996), 290.

Declaration and Address (1809, see Appendix A), reflecting "both the commitment to Christian unity as well as the commitment to base that union on biblical authority (truth)."[42]

Implementing the unity among Christians that is granted by God's grace is a central challenge for Christians today; but the implementation of this challenge is not easy and is faced with danger. True unity is *in Christ*, but today it is not always clear that those in the forefront of unity efforts are fully committed to the Christ as a first priority. As John Cobb, Jr., warns: "Some seem to care more for the victory of a particular program on either the traditionalist or the reformist side than whether that program is faithful to Christ."[43] As the General Assembly of the Church of God (Anderson) rightly stated in 1988: "Any inter-church body involved in a relationship [with ministry structures of the Church of God] should be committed publicly to the divinity and lordship of Jesus Christ. He is central to the meaning and the mission of the church!"[44]

It remains the case that God founded only *one* church (John 10:16; 21:15; Eph. 5:27) and believers are expected to make every effort to maintain its unity in the Spirit (Eph. 4:3-4). The best means for maintaining this unity is still in question; but that means probably relies on several affirmations expressed well by a group of local congregations in England that represent widely differing Christian traditions. They decided to covenant together in 1987 as the "Burnley Lane Fellowship of Churches." Their formal covenant of agreement reads in part:

We the people of Burnley Lane Baptist Church, the

---

[42]James North, *Union In Truth*, xii.

[43]John B. Cobb, Jr., "The Unity of the Church and the Unity of Humanity," *Mid-Stream* 34:1 (January, 1995), 10.

[44]For the full text and context of this statement by the General Assembly, see Barry Callen, *Journeying Together: A Documentary History of the Church of God (Anderson)* (Anderson, IN: Leadership Council of the Church of God and Warner Press, 1996), 38-42.

Church of Christ, New Hall Street, Colne Road Methodist
Church, Elim Methodist Church, St. Andrew's Church of
England, St. Cuthbert's Church of England, St. John the
Baptist, Roman Catholic—repent of our past divisions
which have hindered the proclamation of the Gospel;—
confess our common faith in one God, our Creator,
Sustainer and Saviour, made known to us by his Spirit in
the person of Jesus and in the witness of Scripture;—
acknowledge one another as members of the universal
Church and as brothers and sisters in Christ;—recognize
and rejoice in one another's traditions within the
Christian faith, and respect the calls of obedience which
they make upon us;—believe that we are called to display
the oneness of God in the oneness of our life together so
that all people may come to faith in God and in his
Christ. As God grants us grace, we therefore covenant
together to share our Christian pilgrimage, and to promote in whatever ways we can the visible unity and mission of the Church.[45]

The vision remains. For the sake of the mission of the
church, how can Christians today increase a visible and
meaningful unity among themselves? The quest goes on.
Two bodies of Christians in particular, the Christian
Churches/Churches of Christ and the Church of God
(Anderson) have carried this unity burden since the nineteenth century. In more recent years they have begun
engaging in this quest together.

---

[45]As found in Norris, *The Apostolic Faith*, xxv.

40

Chapter Two

CHALLENGE:
RELEASE FROM MERE RHETORIC

As was amply demonstrated in chapter one, we live in a century that has witnessed the greatest outpouring of ecumenical concern since the founding of the church. Never before has there been so much activity among various denominational bodies in their quest to reestablish the oneness of the church. Part of this high level of activity is simply because never before in the history of the church have there been so many denominations.

A recent listing identified 2,100 different denominations in the United States alone. Many church leaders have become unwilling to tacitly accept this status quo. Through the Ecumenical Movement they have tried to develop opportunities for both discussion and implementation of a greater sense of Christian unity. The Church of God (Anderson) and the Christian Churches/Churches of Christ have tended to refrain from participation in such efforts.[1] This in spite of the fact that the self-understanding of each group would tend to support such ecumenical endeavors. Both groups have had a historic commitment to Christian unity, but both groups have also been lacking

---

[1]See Appendix H for one significant exception.

in having generated significant success in unity efforts. A look at the history of both groups from this perspective might be helpful.

Church of God (Anderson): Efforts Toward Unity

Daniel S. Warner (1842-1895) joined the group known as the General Eldership of Churches of God of North America (often referred to as the Winebrennerians) soon after the Civil War.[2] He served effectively among this body of Christians for about a decade. But when Warner began to identify with the Holiness Movement and experienced "entire sanctification" in 1877, denominational leaders became uncomfortable with him. This culminated in a church trial on January 30, 1878, in which Warner was forced out of the church.[3]

For fellowship and ministry opportunity, Warner soon joined the Northern Indiana Eldership of the Churches of God, a splinter branch of the Winebrennerians. Warner's efforts turned into an editorial vein and by 1881 he was publishing the *Gospel Trumpet*. But in April of that year, while conducting a revival meeting in Indiana, Warner "saw the church."[4] This experience led him to an impatient abandonment of sectarian divisions and the stale status quo of the divided churches. He would now preach holiness but disavow sectarian and denominational divisions. He withdrew from the National Holiness Association because it sanctioned denominational membership and from the Northern Indiana Eldership of the Churches of God because it would not abandon traditional concepts of church membership. Warner declared that he would "come out" from all sectism.[5]

---

[2]For an overview of the life of Warner, we rely heavily on Barry L. Callen, *It's God's Church!*

[3]Ibid., 67-78.

[4]Ibid., 81-93.

[5]Ibid., 93-95.

Other frustrated and visionary Christians responded to the call of Warner and his growing band of colleagues in the unity cause. They continued to lead increasing numbers of people out of sectarian divisions and into God's one church (the church of God composed of all of God's children). After numerous developments and geographical meandering of the home of the Gospel Trumpet Publishing Company (the only organized ministry of this movement in its first decades), by the early twentieth century leadership of the movement finally had concentrated in Anderson, Indiana—and thus the identifying label of Church of God (Anderson). Implicit in the ideology of these early pioneers was the idea of uniting Christians by their withdrawing from sectarianism and rallying around commitment to Jesus Christ instead of around institutional and creedal traditions related to him. As historian Merle Strege states, "Church of God preachers boldly applied the biblical injunction, 'Come out from among them, and be ye separate, saith the Lord' (2 Cor. 6:17) to those living in denominational division."[6]

Unity of the church was believed by these pioneer preachers to be accomplished through a restoration of the biblical experience of holiness and the abandonment of the nonbiblical traditions and divisive creeds and structures of the denominations. This led to a continuing emphasis on "come-outism." All denominations were seen as "sects." Any particular denomination was at best only a part of the Body of Christ. By definition, therefore, all denominations were sects, and "since God's word renounces sects, they cannot be his church."[7] Once a believer had "seen the church" as the whole family of Christ's redeemed and set-apart disciples, continuing membership in a denomination was just as much a sin as theft or adultery. To not flee

---

[6]Merle D. Strege, "The Church of God (Anderson, Indiana): A Historical Introduction" (unpublished paper presented at the Open Forum at Traders Point Christian Church, Indianapolis, IN, March 7, 1989), 11.

[7]Strege, 13, quoting Daniel S. Warner, *The Church of God* (Anderson: Gospel Trumpet Company, n.d.), 27.

these sects of Babylon and "to refrain from 'coming out' placed one's salvation in jeopardy."[8]

Ultimately this "come-outer" spirit accomplishes little in the way of actual unity, despite its ecumenical idealism.[9] Virtually every denomination in existence justifies its claim to be an important and worthy body within the larger Christian family. As the Church of God (Anderson) developed, it made conscientious efforts to carry out its original plea for unity. Along the way this movement's General Assembly and national offices located in Anderson, Indiana, developed the Commission on Christian Unity. When all is said, however, the Church of God (Anderson) has not been especially successful in implementing its goal of achieving Christian unity beyond its own limited boundaries. Lip service to the original plea has often been paid, but the hard coin of reality has not always been congruent to this movement's stated desires.[10] One prominent exception is the unusual level of racial integration that always has been characteristic of the Church of God movement.[11]

Christian Church: Efforts Toward Unity

The Christian Churches trace their origins to a variety of movements on the American frontier about the year 1800. These movements included such leaders as James O'Kelly, coming out of the Methodists in 1792, Elias Smith and Abner Jones, coming out of the Baptists in 1801,

---

[8]Strege, Ibid, 13, quoting Warner, Ibid., 31.

[9]See Barry Callen, "Church of God Reformation Movement (Anderson, Ind.): A Study in Ecumenical Idealism" (masters thesis, Asbury Theological Seminary), 1969.

[10]This movement continues to pursue its vision, with the most recent narrative history of the movement being titled *The Quest for Holiness and Unity* (John W. V. Smith, Warner Press, 1980).

[11]See James Earl Massey, "Race Relations and the American Holiness Movement" in *Wesleyan Theological Journal* 31:1 (Spring 1996), 40-50.

Barton W. Stone, coming out of the Presbyterians in 1804, and Thomas Campbell who left the Presbyterians in 1809.[12] Alexander Campbell, son of Thomas, soon assumed the leadership of the movement begun by his father. All of these movements, though with separate origins, claimed to follow the New Testament alone as their guide, desired the unity of all Christians, and called for other Christians to leave the "sects" and follow the simple faith and practice of New Testament Christianity. Because of this ideology of "restoring" New Testament Christianity, this collective movement is often referred to as the "Restoration Movement."

These disparate groups had some initial success in implementing Christian unity. In various symbolic events in 1811, 1826, and 1841, the O'Kelly, Smith-Jones, and Stone movements united their forces.[13] In 1831/32 the Stone and Campbell Movements achieved a working union as well. Unfortunately it was not a complete success. Alexander Campbell and the leaders of the Smith-Jones movements disagreed over some issues, and the disaffection was undoubtedly exacerbated by personalities. As a result, the Smith-Jones leadership wanted nothing to do with Campbell, and the Stone Movement split between those who united with Campbell's followers and those who remained with the Smith-Jones connection. This latter group (Smith-Jones, O'Kelly, and half of the Stone Movement) soon came to be called the "Christian Connection." They maintained a separate existence until their 1931 union with the Congregational Church, which in turn united with the Evangelical and Reformed Church in 1957 to form the United Church of Christ.[14]

---

[12]For much more detail on all these movements, see James B. North, *Union in Truth: An Interpretive History of the Restoration Movement* (Cincinnati: Standard Publishing Company, 1994).

[13]See James B. North, "Unitive Efforts Between the Christian Church Movements of James O'Kelly, Barton W. Stone, and Elias Smith-Abner Jones," Unpublished MA thesis, Lincoln Christian Seminary, 1963.

[14]For an excellent chart depicting these various groups and their mergers, see Daniel G. Reid (ed.), *Dictionary of Christianity in America*, 1200.

The Stone-Campbell Movement, as it has sometimes been called,[15] prides itself on the union that these two groups achieved in 1832, in spite of the fact that it was far from complete. There were significant differences between the two groups, but they accepted each other and ultimately achieved harmony of practice and thought, even though traces of the different ideologies can still be perceived.[16] One of the confusing leftovers from that union was terminology. The Stone, O'Kelly, and Smith-Jones groups usually called themselves Christian Churches. Stone's group also used the term Church of Christ. Alexander Campbell preferred the label Disciples of Christ. For most of the nineteenth century, the Stone-Campbell Movement used these three terms interchangeably: Christian Church, Church of Christ, Disciples of Christ.

This group continued its quest in a variety of places for a larger measure of Christian unity. Alexander Campbell called for a unity meeting in Lexington in 1841 which had only disappointing attendance and results.[17] The "come-outer" spirit which we noted above in the Church of God movement had its counterpart in the Christian Churches as well. "The sects" were wrong, so people ought to leave such unholy associations, abandon "the denominations" and become simply Christians, that is, join the Restoration Movement. This typically had the effect of saying, "We can have Christian unity if you will leave your denominationalism and become like us." This come-outer spirit did not have any better success for the Christian Churches than it did for the Church of God (Anderson). All movements, even Christian unity movements, have their own historical limitations and thus their own divisive potentials.

---

[15]For instance, Leroy Garrett, *The Stone-Campbell Movement: An Anecdotal History of Three Churches* (Joplin, MO: College Press Publishing Company, 1981).

[16]See North, *Union in Truth*, 155-185.

[17]Ibid., 198-199.

The Campbells had moved into the Baptists in 1815 and remained there until the Baptists began to expel them about 1830. Bitter antagonism often continued, but under Baptist leadership a conference was held between the two groups in 1866. Another meeting in the 1890s saw discussion on Baptist-Disciples union, but with no results. Further serious discussion initiated in 1903 led to many meetings and much discussion until in 1930 the Northern Baptist Convention "rejected the recommendations of its committee that closer cooperation in program and projects be developed with the Disciples."[18]

Because so little was being done within the Christian Churches for the cause of Christian unity, in 1910 Peter Ainslie spoke at the General Convention and gave a stirring call for Disciples to recommit themselves in this regard. He soon led in the formation of a Council on Christian Union. In 1913 the name of this body was changed to the Association for the Promotion of Christian Unity, and ultimately to the Council on Christian Unity.[19] Ainslie was the driving force behind this group for years. The year 1910 also saw the great World Missionary Conference held at Edinburgh, Scotland (see chapter one). Several Disciples attended.

Not only were the Christian Churches failing to achieve Christian unity with other religious groups, they were also moving backwards in their own fellowship. Because of differences over how strictly a position based on biblical silence should be applied to the churches, one large group of churches and leaders broke off in 1906 over the issues of missionary organizations and instrumental music in worship. This latter issue often gives them the name of Noninstrumentalists; they are also called the Churches of Christ. In 1926-1927 discomfort over the

---

[18]Lester G. McAllister and William E. Tucker, *Journey in Faith: A History of the Christian Church (Disciples of Christ)* (Saint Louis: The Bethany Press, 1975), 455-456.

[19]Ibid., 282. Since 1961 the Council on Christian Unity has published *Mid-Stream*, a leading journal of ecumenical dialogue.

inroads of theological liberalism into the Disciples movement led many conservatives to move away from the organized work of the Disciples churches. They formed
competing agencies (missionary sending groups, colleges,
benevolent associations, and a convention) which operated
independently of the organized Disciples work. Thus they
were often called "Independents." More commonly today
they are called the Christian Churches/Churches of
Christ. They are conservative in theology (unlike many of
the Disciples) but use musical instruments in worship
(unlike the Churches of Christ). It is tragic that a movement that began with the commitment to Christian union
now exists in three separate "camps."

Of these three groups, the Disciples have been the most
energetic in ecumenical concerns. As already noted, some
Disciples were present at Edinburgh in 1910. Disciples
were a charter member of the Federal Council of Churches,
later the National Council of Churches and they have been
affiliated with the World Council of Churches. They were
also active in the short-lived Interchurch World Movement
which lasted from 1918 to 1920.[20]

Christian Churches/Churches of Christ: Efforts Toward Christian Unity

The Christian Churches/Churches of Christ (for conve-
nience purposes, hereafter referred to as CC/CC) have not
made any significant movement toward Christian unity
since their separation from the Disciples in the 1920s.
Like the Church of God (Anderson), the "come-outer"
spirit has been their typical methodology for accomplishing Christian unity. As a result there is no lengthy and
admirable record of achievement here.

Things began to change, however, in the 1980s by a
serendipitous development. A few individuals within the

---

[20]Ibid., 348; B. V. Hillis, "Interchurch World Movement," in Reid,
Dictionary of Christianity in America, 576-577.

CC/CC felt that some meeting forum was necessary to discuss challenges facing the Restoration Movement. How could the CC/CC be stimulated again to its original principles? How could younger leadership be developed that would remain committed to these principles, yet be free to implement them in the changing contexts of the future? The CC/CC had a national convention, the North American Christian Convention, but these leaders desired a meeting with a specific focus on these concerns.

A series of annual meetings beginning in 1984 led to often stimulating discussion and interchange on key issues facing the CC/CC. These meetings were called the Open Forum because of the desire to have an openness in discussion and an open microphone which was available to anyone wishing to speak. This was no attempt to control the thinking or direction of the movement. It was a request for involvement and open discussion of issues and challenges.[21]

Because some of these discussions disclosed serious differences in thinking on some key issues—biblical inerrancy, role of women in professional ministry, contemporary worship forms, miraculous gifts—in 1988 the program was slated to discuss movement unity. Speakers were deliberately chosen to address different sides of these issues. A final set of speakers represented the three camps in the larger movement—one from the Churches of Christ, one from the CC/CC, and one from the Disciples.

Dr. Michael Kinnamon, at that time Dean of Christian Theological Seminary in Indianapolis, spoke for the Disciples. In his remarks he challenged the CC/CC to be honest with their alleged concern for unity when they chose instead to stand on the sidelines of the ecumenical dialogue. He said:

---

[21]For a treatment of the development and early history of these Open Forums, see John P. Mills, "A Lesson in Freedom at Work," in Gary E. Weedman (ed.), *Building Up The Church: Scripture, History and Growth: A Festschrift in Honor of Henry E. Webb* (privately printed, 1993), 227-245.

I must admit that my first reaction to tonight's theme was to be utterly overwhelmed by the audacity of it. You ask "How can *we* penetrate other churches with *our* plea for unity?" while around the world churches representing well over a billion Christians are every day engaged in activities aimed at growing in deeper fellowship together! I can't tell you how many conversations I have had through the World Council of Churches with representatives of other churches who wanted to know from me how Independent Christians could be encouraged to join in the search for unity. You see, for most of the Christian world, you are seen as the ones who need to hear the plea— because while you talk about a passion for unity (which other churches share), you remain too often on the sidelines.[22]

As one participant phrased it later, "He nailed our hide to the wall!" There would have to be some release from mere rhetoric on the issue of Christian unity.

Just prior to the 1988 Open Forum, the Convening Committee met and decided to discontinue such meetings. Pre-registrations were less than expected and church leaders seemed to be less than interested. But attendance picked up, and Kinnamon's ringing challenge led to the decision to do something about a wider concept of unity. One of the members of the Convening Committee was the executive director of the North American Christian Convention.[23] Through the Religious Convention Managers' Association he had become acquainted with David Lawson, then Associate General Secretary of the Leadership Council of the Church of God (Anderson, Indiana). The Committee decided to invite the Church of

---

[22]Michael Kinnamon, "Open Forum," photocopied manuscript of a message given at the Open Forum at Chapel Rock Christian Church, Indianapolis, Indiana, March 16, 1988, 2-3. Reproduced in full here as Appendix D.

[23]For a history of this significant annual gathering of thousands of pastoral and lay leaders of the CC/CC, see Edwin Hayden, *North American Gold: The Story of 50 North American Christian Conventions* (Joplin, MO: College Press, 1989).

God to a dialogue at the next Open Forum, to be held in Indianapolis (geographically convenient for both groups) in 1989.[24]

Dialogue Between the Church of God and CC/CC

The resulting 1989 Open Forum was a spiritual highlight for many participants from both fellowships. They quickly discovered that the two church bodies had many things in common. Both groups had a conservative view of Scripture and a commitment to its authority. Both saw themselves as a movements to reform the church according to biblical guidelines. Both had a sincere commitment to Christian unity and baptized only adult believers, and only by the process of immersion. Both rejected denominational structure and emphasized the autonomy of local congregations. Whatever the differences, that seemed enough of a foundation on which to build something potentially significant.

The richness of the fellowship demanded that the association not end here. The Open Forum in 1990 was held in Anderson at the Park Place Church of God. In 1991 another mutual meeting was held in Lexington, Kentucky. In 1993 the meeting was held in conjunction with the Central States Ministers' Convention of the Church of God in St. Joseph, Michigan. In each of these meetings good fellowship predominated and people appreciated the spirit of unity. But there were also major issues to be faced. Numerous areas of agreement existed between the two groups, but significant differences also challenged harmony. Both groups practice baptism by immersion, although the CC/CC understand baptism to be "for remission of sins"; the Church of God does not in exactly the same way (see chapter five). The Church of God approves the ordination of women as ministers; the CC/CC gener-

---

[24]Mills, "A Lesson in Freedom at Work," 242.

ally excludes women from the roles of elder or preaching minister. The Church of God practices footwashing; the CC/CC does not. The CC/CC has local church membership; the Church of God does not.[25]

As a result of these differences, the leadership of the Open Forum decided that substantive discussion of these issues was needed. Scholarly discussion needed to go beyond what was often done in larger public meetings. Thus, since 1992 about half a dozen individuals from each fellowship have been meeting twice a year in Cincinnati to probe these issues. Calling themselves a Task Force on Doctrinal Dialogue, they have written and read scholarly papers and discussed them in detail. They have also prayed together, worshipped together, and continued the discussion about how to develop increased Christian unity between the two groups on behalf of the evangelistic mission of the church. This book is a product of this continuing discussion. The possibility of a volume describing this dialogue process and reporting the results was discussed as early as the 1993 meeting in St. Joseph, Michigan.

Much of the Ecumenical Movement and its subsequent denominational mergers have taken place in a context of religious liberalism. Many conservative and/or evangelical groups have been totally uninterested in the activities of those Christian groups that begin with a liberal presumption concerning the Scriptures. What is unique in the Open Forum discussions is that two groups with conservative commitments about the Bible's nature and role in the Christian life are willing to engage with each other in the give-and-take of ecumenical dialogue. Neither know where this will take them. Members of both groups have some qualms about what may be sacrificed along the way. But both groups are committed to continuing the process. Since the Lord prayed that His people would be one (John 17:21, 23), neither of these two groups wants to become an

---

[25]A fuller treatment of this development and perspective can be found in James B. North and Barry L. Callen, "A Vision in Search of Fulfillment," in *Christian Standard*, February 28, 1993, 4-6.

impediment which would inhibit positive accomplishment of this divine intention. Both groups have said that perhaps the Lord has called us "to the Kingdom for such a time as this" (Esth. 4:14).

The hope of the authors of this book is that these multi-year discussions and their treatment in this volume may stimulate other conservative bodies of Christians to engage in similar dialogue. We humbly want to present ourselves as a "case-in-point" of conservative ecumenical dialogue for the greater glory of the Kingdom of God. It is from the historical context discussed in this chapter and the fervent prayers of those who have participated in it that this volume is sent forth.

Chapter Three

GOAL:
UNITY IN TRUTH, UNITY IN SPIRIT

As we have seen in chapter two, both the Christian Churches/Churches of Christ and the Church of God (Anderson) have had an historic commitment to the ongoing quest for Christian unity. From their different beginnings down to the present, both groups have maintained a faithful resonance with this identifying mark of their traditions. It may be helpful to review some of their formal statements on the subject and then try to analyze their past, present, and future applications.

Church of God (Anderson) Statements on Christian Unity

Daniel S. Warner's original commitment to abandon sectarian and denominational divisions remained with him through the rest of his days. His fervency is reflected in the 1879 proposed consolidation of the Northern Indiana Eldership of the Churches of God and the Evangelical United Mennonite Church. In part Warner's statement read:

We, as the professed sons of God, and members of the United Mennonite church and the Church of God, assembled in the name of Jesus Christ in a joint meeting, do confess it our duty to put away from us every accursed thing that might in the least distract, divide and alienate us in heart or cause divergency in practice; and for the sake of securing an answer to the prayer of the adorable Saviour, we do solemnly agree to abandon anything not warranted by the Word of God and accept any and every thing it teaches. . . . We recognize the Word of God as the only true basis of Christian union.[1]

In 1931 Charles E. Brown, early historian/theologian of the Church of God (Anderson), wrote *A New Approach to Christian Unity* in which he stated several simple steps to achieving authentic Christian unity. "The first formal step necessary to get back to the freedom and unity of the apostolic church is to drop all official creeds." "The second formal step to restore the unity of ancient Christianity is the total abolition of all formal organic denominational divisions among Christian people; not to merge the denominations, but to abolish them is our duty." His third step called for a new focus on Jesus Christ:

The church can only regain her lost visible unity by rallying around our Lord Jesus Christ. In the past there have been cries to rally around this doctrine or that creed, or to rally to this or that battle-cry. Now the call is to come alone to Jesus Christ. . . . Doctrine is very important; but more important it is to get back to the supreme Person, who is the source of all true doctrine.[2]

In addition to these milestone statements from the Church of God tradition, Barry Callen has also compiled other significant statements on unity made more recently by various Church of God individuals and bodies. In 1963,

---

[1]Callen, *It's God's Church!*, 195-196.

[2]Charles E. Brown, *A New Approach to Christian Unity* (Anderson, IN: Warner Press, 1931), 149 ff., quoted in Barry L. Callen (compiler and editor), *Journeying Together: A Documentary History of the Corporate Life of the Church of God Movement (Anderson)* (Anderson: Leadership Council and Warner Press, 1996), 154-156.

for instance, the All-Boards Congress and Planning Council made this statement in its report to the General Assembly of the Church of God:

> We need a strong emphasis on redemptive fellowship in the church. Often our acceptance of other denominations and even members of our own congregations has been conditional, based on whether or not they agreed with "Church of God" thinking. Perhaps we have forgotten the great inclusiveness of "being in Christ."[3]

In 1970 a Consultation of the Church of God recommended several items to the General Assembly. Among them were: "Remain a non-joiner but initiate more conversations with other groups; . . . Officially endorse cooperative endeavors overseas; . . . [and] Share insights on unity wherever doors are open."[4] The 1974 Consultation on Doctrine then examined the theological and historical roots of the Church of God and its pioneers and reported:

> A reexamination of their posture regarding the nature of the church and the role of the Church of God as a reforming movement has given additional evidence that the Church is of God and that God is still working in his church to call sinners to repentance, Christians to unity, and the world to judgment.[5]

In that same year another report to the General Assembly of the Church of God carried this, a part of the "Yokefellow Statement" (the consensus of a recent gathering of Church of God leaders):

> It is our belief that the New Testament sets forth the ideal that all Christians, operating in true humanity, should be able to learn from one another. We maintain, moreover, the conviction that this movement represents a force of reformation leadership within Christendom with

---

[3]Quoted in Callen, *Journeying*, 178.
[4]Ibid., 179.
[5]Ibid.

its emphasis on ecumenicity based on unity rather than on union. To this end, therefore, we encourage through every means possible the establishing and maintaining of work relationships with other like-minded groups on the national, state, and local levels.[6]

In 1979 the faculty and administration of the School of Theology, Anderson University, the North American seminary of the Church of God, published this *We Believe* statement:

> The dividedness among Christian people today is not just unfortunate; it is inappropriate and wholly unacceptable. Unity is clearly God's will for the church. . . . The goal is less a contrived peace treaty among deeply divided church organizations and more a radical reconsideration of what is an appropriate network of relationships among brothers and sisters in Christ.[7]

In April of 1984 the Consultation on Mission and Ministry of the Church of God, meeting in Indianapolis to attempt to set major goals for the Church of God movement to the end of the twentieth century, emphasized the task of the church if it is to really function as the church. One of its stated goals for the movement was

> to expand ministries through voluntary relationships with Christian groups outside the Church of God Reformation Movement and seek to live out the vision of unity through broader interdependent relationships that serve mutual needs for training, fellowship, and witness.[8]

Then in 1985 the Committee on Long Range Planning and Executive Council of the Church of God issued a report to the General Assembly in June which supported

> the historical stance of the Church of God Reformation Movement to seek intentional inter-church relationships

---

[6]Ibid.
[7]Ibid.
[8]Ibid., 180.

through which its own ministries are strengthened and which provide opportunity for the Church of God Reformation Movement to live out its message of Christian unity through enriching the entire Body of Christ.[9]

The General Assembly in 1988 adopted a resolution on Inter-Church Cooperation which stated: "Inter-church relationships should be seen as opportunities to serve and witness in light of the distinctive heritage of the Church of God reformation movement. We have something important to share as well as receive in any such relationship." That same year the General Assembly endorsed a mission statement for the Church of God, calling this movement "to build up the whole body of Christ in unity." Then in 1995 the Leaders' Visioning Retreat asserted that the Church of God exists to "Celebrate the Unity of the Body of Christ."[10]

Throughout all of this the reader can sense the concern for Christian unity that pulsates throughout the Church of God (Anderson). Its history, development, and current identity all reflect this commitment. Yet this one movement is not alone in this concern. The Christian Churches/Churches of Christ share this concern as well.

Christian Churches/Churches of Christ Statements on Christian Unity

B.W. Stone and other leaders of the Stone Movement dissolved the Springfield Presbytery in 1804 when they discerned that their existence as a presbytery was a barrier to the very union for which they were pleading. In the unique *Last Will and Testament of the Springfield Presbytery*, these Christians stated their intention to eliminate themselves as such a barrier: "We *will*, that this body die, be dissolved, and sink into union with the Body

---

[9]Ibid.
[10]Ibid.

59

of Christ at large; for there is but one body."[11] This same document said the participants would "unite with all Christians."[12] The document closed with this statement:

> We heartily unite with *our Christian brethren of every name*, in thanksgiving to God for the display of his goodness in the glorious work he is carrying on in our Western country, which we hope will terminate in the universal spread of the gospel, and the unity of the church.[13]

The Stone Movement was not alone in its commitment to Christian unity. Thomas Campbell, in writing the *Declaration and Address* in 1809, voiced the same commitment. Proposition One of that document emphatically stated: "The Church of Christ upon earth is essentially, intentionally, and constitutionally one."[14] At the conclusion of thirteen propositions, Campbell boldly asserted: "To prepare the way for a permanent Scriptural unity among Christians . . . is, at least, the sincere intention of the above propositions."[15]

Thomas' son Alexander shared these commitments and soon assumed leadership over what came to be called the Campbell Movement. In 1815 the Campbells were accepted by the local Baptists in western Pennsylvania and continued to work among the Baptists as long as the Baptists allowed the Campbells such participation, which was until about 1830. When Alexander Campbell was questioned about his relationship to the Baptists, he admitted that he was in "full communion" with them. He went on to say:

---

[11]"The Last Will and Testament of the Springfield Presbytery," in *The Biography of Eld. Barton Warren Stone*, edited by John Rogers (Cincinnati: J.A. & U.P. James, 1847), 51.

[12]Ibid., 55.

[13]Ibid. Emphasis added.

[14]Thomas Campbell, "Declaration and Address," in *Historical Documents Advocating Christian Union*, edited by Charles Alexander Young (Chicago: The Christian Century Company, 1904), 107-108.

[15]Ibid., 115.

I have no idea of adding to the catalogue of new sects. This game has been played too long. I labor to see sectarianism abolished, and *all Christians of every name* united upon the one foundation upon which the apostolic church was founded.[16]

If Isaac Errett, editor of *The Christian Standard,* carried the mantle of editorial leadership of what came to be the Christian Churches/Churches of Christ after the death of Alexander Campbell in 1866, James H. Garrison, editor of *The Christian-Evangelist,* carried the mantle after the death of Errett in 1888. Around the turn of the century Garrison wrote a pamphlet entitled "The World's Need of our Plea." He summarized two great contributions of the original leaders of the movement. They were the emphasis on Christian unity and a "more rational method of treating the Holy Scriptures."[17] He explained that Alexander Campbell applied Baconian investigation and fact-gathering to understand the Bible. Garrison concluded:

Out of this free and independent method of Biblical study, there resulted a more scriptural, reasonable and consistent view of the whole subject of conversion—involving the nature and office of faith, its relation to the Gospel and to obedience, the work of the Spirit, his mode of operation, the nature of repentance, the place of baptism, and its relation to forgiveness of sins—which, next to the plea for union, we regard as the most important contribution which the current Reformation has made to the religious thought of the age.[18]

Pleas for unity were not limited to the founders of the CC/CC or their first generation of followers. Such pleas continued down through the decades. James DeForest

---

[16]Alexander Campbell, in *The Christian Baptist,* Vol. III, No. 7 (February, 1826) [Gospel Advocate Reprint Edition, 1955], 146. Emphasis added.

[17]James Harvey Garrison, "The World's Need of Our Plea," in Young, *Historical Documents,* 352.

[18]Ibid., 353.

Murch in his path-breaking history *Christians Only* quoted P.H. Welshimer writing in an article in the *Christian Standard* in 1927:

> So long as the people have the same creed—which is Christ—recognize the inspiration of the Scriptures, take Christ as their authority and the Scripture as the Revelation of that authority, adhere to the New Testament ordinances, and make Christians in the New Testament way, they will be united. . . .
>
> [Loyal Disciples] are a thousand times more concerned with restoring the church of the New Testament in the whole earth than they are about Christian unity, for when the church of the New Testament obtains everywhere, automatically, the desired union will be present.[19]

Murch's penultimate chapter is entitled "Modern Disciples and Christian Unity." His final chapter deals with the Restoration Plea in an ecumenical era. He ends the book with a page-long "Prayer for Unity."[20]

In his 1990 history of the Restoration Movement, or the Stone-Campbell tradition, Henry E. Webb devotes his first chapter to detailing the "mandate of the movement," the concern for unity that has marked the Movement since its beginning. Toward the end of that initial chapter he states:

> The Restoration Movement, whose history is presented in this volume, could be viewed as simply another in the long series of restoration efforts in the history of the church. To do so would be to miss its uniqueness and do it a grave injustice. Generally, movements of this type have viewed restoration as a desired end in itself. The movement under study has rather viewed the restoration of New Testament Christianity as an effective means for the

---

[19]James DeForest Murch, 355. The brackets beginning the second paragraph are in Murch's text. The term "Disciples" would not now be used as referring to conservative members of the CC/CC, although this was still common in Murch's era.

[20]Ibid., 375.

62

achievement of another end, namely the unity of the fractured body of followers of Christ.[21]

James North, in his history of the CC/CC published in 1994, emphasized throughout the volume what he called the twin roots of the Restoration Movement, the concerns for biblical authority and Christian unity. He concluded the volume with this introspective plea:

> What are we willing to do to see the Restoration Movement accomplish its long term goals—not the erection of an identifiable fellowship, but the unity of the world according to the prayer of Jesus as recorded in John 17: that we may be one that the world may be won.[22]

Thus, it is evident that the CC/CC is as historically committed to the plea for Christian unity as is the Church of God. Throughout their histories both groups have consistently articulated this crucial element of their respective movement identities. As the twentieth century closes, both groups are seeking anew to reclaim this common heritage for the sake of today's church and world—and to do it together.

Where Should All This Lead?

We have seen that both the Church of God and the CC/CC have often put into print their plea for and commitment to Christian unity. Yet merely preaching and publishing this plea is not enough. It is important that it be put into practice. That is the primary reason why both groups have continued to hold various discussion meetings for the past eight years—initially in the Open Forum, then continuing in the Task Force on Doctrinal Dialogue. A great deal of effort, financial investment, and prayer have gone into these many meetings. Both groups feel that the experience has been worth the personal expenditure of time and effort.

---

[21]Henry E. Webb, *In Search of Christian Unity*, 37-38.

[22]James B. North, *Unity in Truth*, 369.

What is the result? Will the two groups finally merge? Probably not, unless God should will otherwise. Both groups have often joked about the "M" word, but neither group has any such goal in mind (unless, of course, the "M" is intended to begin the word "ministry" or "mission" and not merger). One of the leaders involved in the meetings talked about the two groups "courting" each other, even jokingly referred to the possibility that they were living together, but that there was no wedding planned!

How then are we to assess all this effort? Is it only hype? Is it only a verbal genuflection toward the altar of unity while our hearts are committed to the contrary? We trust not. An understanding of all this involves a further exploration of what these two movements mean by "unity."

Chapter four of this volume details some of the practical ministry cooperation that has occurred between the two groups both before and during these discussions. A working sense of unity may be a sense of working together for the common cause of the Kingdom of God, a functional togetherness not necessarily leading to any institutional results. Some participants have been content with this; others have voiced the desire for something more organic in the way of measurable unity. There has not been unanimity on how this is to be conceived or achieved. The differences of perspective here are not necessarily a division of expectation between the Church of God on the one hand and the CC/CC on the other. The differences often cut through both groups. There is a certain inability to agree on where all this should lead.

Perhaps this confusion should be not seen as unexpected or even undesirable. More is involved than two fellowships striving to attain a greater measure of commonness in the body of Christ. Both groups are made up of numerous individuals, many of whom have different perspectives. This diversity may be inescapable, and thus it ought to be admitted and possibly even celebrated. We do not have to be twins to be brothers and sisters!

In their book *Systems-Sensitive Leadership: Empowering Diversity Without Polarizing the Church,* Michael C. Armour and Don Browning deal with various attitudes that characterize differing "styles" of church leadership. Perhaps some of their insights can be useful here. Using the terminology of Dr. Clare Graves, a professor of developmental psychology from Union College in New York, Armour and Browning categorize eight "systems." Each of these systems is a way of looking at things—something like a mindset. Graves identifies eight of these systems, ranging from a more primitive and narrowly focused worldview to a much more complex one. What follows is a very reduced summation of Armour and Browning's treatment of these systems.[23] We need not look at all the systems, only at those most applicable to our immediate interest and application.

System Three is a dominant system that is control oriented. There is an authoritative leader and all others are followers. System Four reacts to the authoritarian control of System Three. It searches for truth—"harmony on the basis of shared beliefs."[24] This system also builds institutions and cultivates institutional loyalty. As a result there are often rules and regulations, plus a bureaucracy. There is a control mentality from the top down, although it is based on shared beliefs, not just on the power mentality of System Three.

System Five promotes more of a desire to achieve. "It has little patience with policies and structures that hamper what it perceives as needed change."[25] It supports institutions only as far as they provide personal fulfillment and the attainment of satisfactory objectives. It does not reflect deep devotion to theological structures, but

---

[23]For a fuller treatment, see Michael C. Armour and Don Browning, *Systems-Sensitive Leadership: Empowering Diversity Without Polarizing the Church* (Joplin, MO: College Press Publishing Company, 1995).

[24]Ibid., 77.

[25]Ibid., 89.

favors creativity and innovation in planning and a personal "walk with the Lord."

System Six to a certain extent is a response to the previous three. It reacts negatively to the power elitism of System Three, the class elitism of System Four, and the success elitism of System Five. It wants to bring healing and unity to the entire community. It seeks out interpersonal settings and wants genuine fellowship. Unfortunately, System Six also carries with it the tendency to alienate the other systems with a "holier than thou" attitude. In the name of being inclusive and healing it can be intolerant of the sensitivities of the other systems. This often earns it the suspicion of Systems Three and Four which are more oriented to authoritarian power (which System Six despises) or doctrinal constructs (which it distrusts).

We have mentioned this "systems" approach because it may well illustrate some of the difficulties the Church of God and the CC/CC experience as they seek to conceive the goal and "style" of Christian unity and participate in this continuing dialogue. One difficulty is that the two groups tend to represent different temperamental systems. The CC/CC historically has seen a particular "pattern" to the apostolic church and has tried to replicate that pattern in today's world as much as is possible. This is somewhat of a System Four approach. There is a concern for wholeness and unity, but it is to conform to the institutional pattern of apostolic Christianity. There is a proper "form" thought to be biblical and basic.

The Church of God, meanwhile, historically has placed more emphasis on the centrality of the "experience" of regeneration, conversion, and holiness. This is more of a System Five approach. Institutional structures are not as meaningful. That is one reason why the CC/CC always has churches structured under a group of elders, while the Church of God has been open to a variety of patterns of congregational governance. This may not be a "clash" of systems, but it does create an atmosphere of recognized difference that brings some wariness and hesitancy.

A second difficulty that the "systems" approach highlights is one that cuts across (not between) these two fellowships. There are System Four individuals in both
movements who are leery of the inter-movement dialogue
because it seems to jeopardize the doctrinal position or
distinctive heritage that each group has had. These
System Four people are loyal to the institution—an institution which they see as having successfully created a
religious community which is both faithful to God and
sensitive to people's needs. Because the two groups do
have some differences in doctrine and in practice, System
Four individuals are wary of any talk of unity. They see it
as an invitation to compromise, a potential sell-out, a
threatened abandonment of what their particular movement has always stood and worked for.

System Five people, on the other hand, do not want to be
limited by the institutional baggage of their heritage. They
want to move on to successful implementation of the goals—
unity being a common one for both groups. Thus they want
to see movement, achievement, even if it means alienating
Systems Four individuals (whom they tend to see as nonpro-
ductive people anyway). They want to establish joint commissions to implement unity by planning cooperative
activity which will lead to a larger achievement of unity of
spirit. If there are any "merger-minded" people in either of
these church bodies, they would be in System Five.

System Six people carry many of the same concerns,
including the desire to abandon institutional baggage.
They want unity of spirit, but they feel no compunction to
work out details of operation. They are content with a har-
monious spirit of working together, cooperating in common
tasks, not worrying about such things as institutional
identity, institutional loyalty, or doctrinal correctness. Such
structural precision is considered secondary to the much
more important task of harmoniously demonstrating unity
and freeing people to discover their own network of relationships. Theirs is not a "merger mentality" as much as a
cooperative spirit of fellowship and brotherhood.

More Whole When Together

Thus the dialogue continues between these two movements committed to Christian unity. Where exactly it is headed no one knows; in fact, different people certainly have different ideas about where they believe it ought to go. There is no consensus. Given the disparate nature of the memberships of these two fellowships, there probably will never be consensus on such an issue. But at least a majority of both groups feel the commitment to continue the process. Perhaps in so doing the Holy Spirit can work beyond our abilities and insecurities and achieve something that none of us can envision at the moment. We feel the challenge of the Spirit calling us to a greater measure of unity. We want to be faithful to that call.

An incident that occurred at the Open Forum in 1988 (before the Church of God was participating) may highlight another need. Two individuals from the CC/CC were discussing the issue of biblical inerrancy. One was arguing that if the Bible is errant, then there is no established authority; giving up the principle of inerrancy means going down the "slippery slope" into dependence merely on human rationalism. The other individual was pointing out that the term "inerrant" is not a biblical view; it is possible to have a "high view" of Scripture without insisting on inerrancy; to insist on it is to go down the "slippery slope" of narrow doctrinal scholasticism. In one of the small group sessions, however, a third individual pointed out that the imagery of "slippery slopes" suggests that one person is at the peak of the mount while others are not. It may be, he observed, that neither group is at the peak; both groups are somewhat down from the peak and in danger of sliding down their respective sides. They need to hang on to each other and thus save themselves from sliding down the slopes as well as save their brothers and sisters on the other side from their downward slide.

Perhaps this also is true in relation to this present process of dialogue on behalf of Christian unity. It may be that the Church of God and the CC/CC need each other to balance their views and achieve a greater wholeness that neither can know otherwise. If the CC/CC is inclined too much toward Enlightenment rationalism and the Church of God is too much inclined toward subjective spiritual experiences, then perhaps both need each other and thus can keep each other from sliding down their respective slopes.

This analysis may have a wider application than just to the Church of God and the CC/CC. We invite others to reflect seriously on their own situations and investigate what can be done through their own fellowships to be more faithful to Christ's desire for our unity as diverse believers in the same Christ. Other fellowships have additional perspectives that can make positive contributions to the quest for unity and wholeness, and keep even more groups from sliding down into narrowly focused error. It is in this humble spirit that the whole enterprise of this present dialogue has been undertaken, and particularly that this volume has been written. Perhaps others can achieve what we have only begun. Perhaps others can lead the way to a deeper, more vital understanding and practice of New Testament unity. Such is our prayer and fondest dream.

Chapter Four

PATH:
OUR JOURNEY THUS FAR

Especially appropriate and helpful is putting in "journey" terms the process and current status of the ongoing dialogue and ministry relationships between the Christian Churches/Churches of Christ and the Church of God (Anderson). Note, for instance, the following wisdom attributed to Martin Luther:

> This life, therefore, is not righteousness, but growth in righteousness, not health, but healing, not being, but becoming, not rest, but exercise. We are not yet what we shall be, but we are growing toward it, the process is not yet finished, but it is going on; this is not the end, but it is the road. All does not yet gleam in glory, but all is being purified.

A coming-together-in-Christ journey has begun. It remains incomplete and in process. It is not an end in itself, but it is a good and right road.

A Meeting of Two Movements

In the nineteenth century two different Christian movements began that had a common dream. They hoped that all children of God would come together in unity and work for the perfection and mission of God's people under the authority and guidance of biblical teaching. They looked with new hope to the earliest generations of the church to see again and approach a fresh realization of the originating essence of the Christian faith; and they looked with deep sadness at the many centuries of the church's significant departure from its originating essence.

These two reforming movements—one symbolized by the leadership of Alexander Campbell, the other inspired in large part by pioneer Daniel S. Warner—became significant bodies of believers as they grew and matured. Congregations of the Christian Churches/Churches of Christ and the Church of God (Anderson) soon dotted the entire American landscape as well as spreading to many other countries. Leaders such as Campbell and Warner shared a similar vision of Christian unity, but the two movements they represented have remained apart.

Recently that awkward separation has been changing. For the last year, ministers of these two movements have been meeting together in Cincinnati, Ohio, to share their vision of the church, talk about mutual problems of local ministry, and learn about each other's strengths and idiosyncrasies. They have eaten together, prayed, joined in fellowship, and even argued together, and have planned joint worship times. The goal of all this has been to bring to fuller realization the prayer of Jesus that "they all may be one" (John 17:21).

In 1989, national meetings began to occur between leaders of the Christian Churches/Churches of Christ and the Church of God (Anderson). These meetings became known as the "Open Forum." The Open Forum actually began in 1984 as a brainstorming effort within the Christian Churches/Churches of Christ about how to get their congregations out of a lethargic plateau they were then experiencing. A number of individuals decided to call for a meeting of representative key leaders in the Christian Churches/Churches of Christ to probe ways to

72

restore real "movement" into what is fondly called the "Restoration Movement"—a movement to restore New Testament Christianity to today's splintered denominational world.

After several successful meetings where issues of importance were discussed, members of the Church of God (Anderson) were invited in 1989 to come to Traders Point Christian Church in Indianapolis to worship together and discuss issues of common interest in church history, theology, practice, and the ordinances. What emerged from this first meeting was the realization that both groups have an overwhelming number of essential elements in common. Additional meetings involving hundreds of persons now have convened in Anderson, Indiana, in 1990 and in Lexington, Kentucky, in 1991. These friendly meetings have not been shallow and nonconfrontive, however. In spite of the numerous similarities acknowledged by the Christian Churches/Church of God (Anderson), there are still some significant differences between them.

Because of the differences, leaders in the national gatherings decided in 1991 that provision should be made for the scholarly, in-depth discussion of these issues, getting beyond the exploratory conversations held in the much larger Open Forum meetings. In August of that year, a Task Force on Doctrinal Dialogue gathered in Cincinnati, composed of equal numbers of individuals from the two groups. Formal papers were presented from both groups in this and subsequent meetings (see bibliography below). Numerous other gatherings and joint activities for mutual understanding and cooperative ministry also have occurred (see select listing below).

More of the history of this dialogue's beginning is found in chapter two. The goal of this present chapter, however, is to review some of the tentative results. Beyond abstract discussion of theological issues, these many meetings and new relationships have manifested a primary concern for the evangelistic mission of the church. A persistent question has been, "In what ways can these two movements join together in common work for the advancement of the kingdom of God on earth?"[1]

Symbols of the Goal

The story is well told by noting the journeys of two men. They are friends and now symbols, fellow workers in the common cause of Christ. They are two church leaders who began their young lives together in the same small town and high school, went their separate ways, and many years later, partially through the work of the Open Forum between the Christian Churches/Churches of Christ and the Church of God (Anderson), have found each other again. Their story helps show the meaning of the larger story of the Open Forum itself.

The little Kansas town is called Hugoton. In the early 1950s two young men graduated from the town's high school. Bob Wetzel graduated in 1952 and was active with his family in the local congregation of the Christian Church. Gary Ausbun graduated the next year and was active with his family in the local congregation of the Church of God (Anderson). This was a small farming town in Western Kansas, population about 2,000. These two young men were both Christians, played football together, and shared in some church youth activities, although their two congregations were separate and did not interact very much outside the boundaries of their own fellowships.

Following high school, both Bob and Gary went on to college. Bob attended Midwest Christian College in Oklahoma City and then went on to the University of Nebraska for his graduate education. Gary received an athletic scholarship to Fort Hays Kansas State College, but after one year felt a calling to Christian ministry, transferred to Anderson University in Indiana, graduating

---

[1]An earlier version of this section was published as a news release both in *Christian Standard* and *Vital Christianity* in February, 1993, seeking to inform to that date wider circles in both movements about this Open-Forum dialogue.

from its college in 1958 and its School of Theology in 1962.

Both of these men became respected leaders in their respective movements, although their paths no longer crossed very often. Then in 1993 that changed, if only briefly. They were brought together again in Hugoton, Kansas, for the fortieth year reunion of the high school class. While home for this occasion, each, in the spirit of the Open Forum, was asked by the respective pastor of the other movement's local congregation to fill the pulpit, teach Sunday School, and share about the respective uniqueness of the two movements they represented. The subtle wall of separation was being breached.

Another breaching of such a wall has occurred in Southern California, especially on the campus of Pacific Christian College. This unifying trend is symbolized well by the person of Dr. Leroy Fulton. Having served for many years as president of Warner Southern College in Florida (Church of God), in the most recent years Dr. Fulton has functioned in a senior administrative role at Pacific Christian College. He has preached in numerous congregations of the Christian Churches/Churches of Christ in the Western states and become an enthusiastic linking person between these two Christian fellowships, helping to encourage and implement the following (examples only):

1. Pacific Christian College has established a Church of God heritage collection in its library, received into the membership of its Board of Directors Rev. Robert Pearson, Executive Director of the Association of the Church of God in Southern California, and in 1996 granted an honorary doctorate to Rev. Benjamin Reid, then pastor of a large congregation of the Church of God in Los Angeles.

2. Three preaching clinics have been sponsored jointly by Pacific Christian College and the Association of the Church of God in Southern California, with various Church of God meetings hosted on campus.

Individuals make a difference. Many have made deep commitments to the ongoing dialogue between the

Christian Churches/Churches of Christ and the Church of God (Anderson). John Mills of Ohio and David Lawson of Indiana deserve special note in this regard.

What We Have Learned Together

Those church leaders who have participated actively in this dialogue process have learned to know new brothers and sisters in the faith and much about a parallel Christian tradition previously known to them in name only. Out of this rich learning context have come a series of other learnings worthy of note.

1. *This Process Is Worth the Time*. The last thing any of us needs is more busywork, more routine and maybe unnecessary tending to organizational machinery. All of us are busy people and have to be convinced that such a new venture as this multi-year "Open Forum" process with the Christian Churches/Churches of Christ is not just more meetings and endless talk. Dialogue participants have dealt directly with the question, "Is it all really worthwhile?" Although the final verdict is not in, most of the participants have developed a growing conviction that this process may be ordered of God for some important ends. We judge it most worthwhile, even though many specifics of potential outcomes still are seen only dimly, if at all.

2. *Historical Perspective Increases One's Humility*. The Church of God movement, especially in its early decades, tended to dismiss as without value much of Christian church history. That history was seen mostly as centuries of apostasy now about to end with the gathering of God's true church and the return of Christ. In the train of bold reformers like Martin Luther and John Wesley, movement leaders rejoiced in the belief that God was introducing again the "early morning light." We saw ourselves being called to "cleanse the sanctuary" in a full and final way as the age was coming to a close. So it has been easy for us as a movement to value A.D. 50 and A.D. 1880, while generally lamenting most in between as a sorry state of affairs.

There now is a growing realization of the loss we have sustained by devaluing the long and rich "restorationist" tradition of which the movement is a part. Particularly in the United States, the Stone/Campbell tradition predated the Church of God movement and is full of common cause with it. There are some differences, to be sure. Some of these differences can be an enrichment to the movement. Why? In part because, in addition to any distinctiveness granted the Church of God movement by divine grace, the movement also is a product of a given time and place in church history. That time and place inevitably have had a significant shaping influence, an influence we have only begun to understand. Sharing with a dialogue partner who has so much in common with us sharpens our historical perspective and thereby enhances our self-understanding.

We have learned that the roles played by the Enlightenment and American Holiness/Revivalism have shaped the theological perspectives of our respective heritages. This awareness now influences our attitude and helps us to transcend certain limitations coming from our histories.[2]

3. *We Too Have Some Walls*. Church of God participants in the Open Forum have learned that the structural and non-structural obstacles to real Christian unity are more subtle and complex than sometimes we have assumed. We all live in a day when traditional denominational walls are eroding rapidly. Nevertheless, even free-church "restorationist" bodies that champion non-creedalism and Christian unity visions often themselves develop significant and stubborn "denominational" characteristics (products of humanity and history). We certainly appreciate and learn from the historic Christian creeds,

---

[2]The exact wording of this paragraph was affirmed by all participants of the Task Force on Doctrinal Dialogue at its meeting in April, 1996, in Cincinnati. See Appendix I, pp. 213-214.

but we are unwilling to make the exact wording of any of these creeds a test of Christian fellowship.

4. *We Need To Practice What We Preach*. Why did some Church of God leaders become involved in this particular dialogue process? The answer is more than the fact that there was an opportunity and a direct invitation from leaders of the Christian Churches/Churches of Christ. For many decades our movement has set forth what we have judged to be the New Testament vision of Christian unity. We have declared our willingness to "reach our hands in fellowship to every bloodwashed one." Sometimes over the decades we have been accused of being sectish ourselves, not living up to our proclaimed ideal. In fact, we have not always modeled clearly what we have announced with the best of intentions.

At first it was natural for our movement to focus on being critical of the obvious wrongs seen all across the denominationalized and demoralized Christian community. The positive building of a viable alternative, however, always is more difficult than the negative judging of what is so wrong. Some of us in the movement have learned only slowly that it is difficult to preach convincingly a commitment-based and fellowship-based vision of Christian unity without being intentional about seeking its actualization. Together, we clearly desire to recover for our time the essence of New Testament Christianity.

5. *Both Groups Resist the "M" Word*. Participants in this dialogue process have reminded each other over these last years that the "M" word, *merger*, is not on the Open Forum agenda. A structural uniting of our two church bodies is not our priority goal. We all know that immediate mistrust and spirited opposition would arise from within each of our constituencies if it were perceived that these dialogues were exploring seriously anything like a "denominational" merger. Neither body envisions such a union outcome as the way to achieve Christian unity. Neither body has a structure to make such a thing possible even if it were desirable. We have learned, nonetheless, that a certain "flowing together" is a possibility, probably even in some sense a divinely guided goal. Such meshing should focus on building relationships, enriching understandings, and discovering cooperative ministry opportunities.

We have become convinced that there are many important things that we and the Christian Churches/Churches of Christ can do to help each other in church life and mission. Without raising the specter of a "merger mentality," we can do much together to further the Kingdom's cause. We have learned, however, that moving over this fruitful frontier, whatever its components might turn out to be, will require a selfless attitude, and certainly an avoidance of "turf protection" by our several church institutions. History teaches that, right as it may be, this cooperative path is narrow and traveled successfully only by a few.

6. *Mission Is the Motive That Inspires Our Dialogue*. Merger is not the goal, and a bad conscience about poor performance in past unity efforts did play a key role in beginning this dialogue process. The primary motive driving and sustaining this dialogue, however, has been a mutual concern for the better accomplishment of Christian mission. Mission is the motive. Mission is accomplished best in cooperation with brothers and sisters in Christ. The church is bigger than "us." Its mission will get done best when we are open to doing it together.

7. *We Have Much To Learn If We Remain Open*. Driven by our commitment to accomplishing the church's mission, the Church of God participants in this dialogue have tended to learn one or two theological lessons in the process. One is that the movement should take more seriously its own stance of non-creedalism. The challenge for us is not to protect our current perceptions of truth (one way to define denominationalism) so much as it is to continue seeking the most adequate possible apprehension of truth in an open fellowship of maturing believers. Openness and maturing do not survive well in a context of defensiveness and suspicion. It is enabled by widening the circle of disciples who are searching for all that God intends for the whole church to know and be and do. Much overblown has been our movement's historic fear of theological contamination if we should involve ourselves seriously with Christians whose perspectives differ at points from our own. Some of us now are learning that we ought to believe more strongly that truth is not that fragile and that God still superintends the life of his faithful people. In the end, it is not light that yields to darkness, but darkness to light.

We as two church movements have much with which to enrich each other. We have begun to learn from each other and must continue to benefit by building meaningful relationships. While we hold in common the lordship of Jesus Christ, we do not need to arrive at full consensus on doctrinal issues in order to be open to each other, influenced by each other, genuinely valuing and loving each other, and learning to minister with each other.[3]

8. *Baptism: Study of an Apparent Doctrinal Difference*. Neither body involved in this Open Forum process is creedal in nature, nor by tradition is either "fundamentalist" in the rigid, doctrinaire sense of this term. Doctrinal positions, nonetheless, have been explored in considerable detail, with only a few found to be stubbornly troublesome between us. Theological "style" and emphasis occasionally vary between our groups, mostly products of our differing histories of origin. A key reason appears to be the impact of aspects of the "Enlightenment" on one group and the more experience-oriented impact of American revivalism on the other.

The doctrinal dialogue portion of the Open Forum often has focused its attention on the subject of Christian baptism. Both groups believe baptism to be a biblical

---

[3]The exact wording of this paragraph was affirmed by all participants of the Task Force on Doctrinal Dialogue at its meeting in April, 1996, in Cincinnati.

mandate and best administered by immersion. We agree that genuine repentance of sin is required prior to baptism, thus making this sacred practice not appropriate for infants. We agree further that there is no merit leading to salvation in the baptismal mechanics themselves—baptism is not what saves. With all this agreement, however, one key area related to baptism remains unresolved. Our dialogue partner tends to see the phrase "for the remission of sins" necessarily related closely to baptism, although by this association not meaning "baptismal regeneration." We have explored why the retention of this phrase with baptism is seen as so crucial by one group and why it is a matter of substantial concern for the other. Language certainly is one problem. Time and patient listening are required to really hear and understand each other here. But language is not all of the problem.

One insight we have gained has been of some help. Our differing approaches to baptism and "the remission of sins," obviously a biblical phrase, can be explained in part by the differing "enemies" each group has been fighting over the decades. The Christian Churches/Churches of Christ is a movement that has been resisting "faith-only" revivalism and "liberalism" as represented to them by the Disciples of Christ wing of the restorationist movement. "For the remission of sins" has become a touchstone in their eyes for strict biblical obedience. The Church of God, on the other hand, has been resisting Roman Catholicism and her "Protestant daughters." Our movement has been very sensitive about anything that appears to retain for establishment Christianity a control over the dispensing of God's grace through given church rites, including baptism.

The April, 1996, meeting in Cincinnati of the Task Force on Doctrinal Dialogue developed a statement on the status of the doctrinal conversations that had been in progress for several years between the Christian Churches/Churches of Christ and the Church of God.[4] To

---

[4]See Appendix I for the full text of this statement of theological consensus.

the surprise and delight of the participants, an affirmation on baptism was made that could be agreed to by all present. It read:

> We are agreed that baptism is commanded by the Lord Jesus to be practiced by all of His followers. This baptism is to be by the immersion in water of penitent believers. Baptism is symbolic of the atoning death, burial, and resurrection of Christ. By its nature as well as by biblical teaching, baptism is involved with forgiveness of sin. We take pains, however, to repudiate any doctrine of baptismal regeneration, holding that forgiveness is wholly a matter of God's grace.

9. *We Suffer a Common Dilemma*. Both dialogue bodies have the dilemma of freedom-spontaneity versus efficiency-accountability in church life. Both groups resist a denominationalizing trend, but also seek some path to more efficiency and mutual accountability. Here is a central dilemma we share, one not easily resolved. While neither of us wants any more church structure, both are searching for better ways to be accountable and effective. No one has yet arrived at the ideal place. Are there ways that we can assist each other along this uncharted path? We are learning that there are.

10. *Testimony Is a Good Strategy*. A productive way to proceed in demonstrating the potential meaningfulness of this Open Forum is to take local and practical action. In Cincinnati, Ohio, for instance, pastors and spouses from each of these church groups now have become acquainted and mutually supportive. Professors and administrators from some Church of God schools have met some of their counterparts. Visits and guest lectures across group lines have begun. Such developments are encouraging and might be repeated elsewhere with good benefit. All of these Open Forum meetings and talk are helpful only when real relationships evolve and prove productive for the Kingdom of God. Some good things have happened and need to be told widely.

11. *Each Group Is Challenged To Widen the Dialogue Circle.* More dialogue participants are invited and more wisdom is needed. The bottom line is this—two similar groups of God's children have begun an honest quest for a fuller realization of the divine will for our day. The goal is elusive, but since it seems divinely motivated, the quest goes on.

What We Have Accomplished Together

It is apparent that these years of discussion and mutual effort have been productive. We have developed a mutual appreciation and trust in our times together. We have discovered a broad expanse of consensus in our common faith and work and have expanded the number of persons who have firsthand acquaintance with the dialogue.

Beyond increased acquaintance and much writing and talking, we have found ways to be on mission together. Here are a few.

1. The Missionary Board of the Church of God has cooperated with the mission work of the Christian Churches/Churches of Christ to prepare a missionary couple to serve unreached peoples.

2. In Africa the Missionary Board of the Church of God, through its official registration, was able to assist the local Christian Churches' mission to conserve equipment and property which otherwise would have been lost.

3. Some neighboring congregations of these two fellowships in the United States have found ways to work together. They have had unity services, shared facilities, formed support groups among pastors and spouses, constructed a Habitat For Humanity house as a joint congregational project, etc. Prime examples of inter-congregational cooperation have been in Canton and Cincinnati, Ohio.

4. A Joliet, Illinois, Christian Church congregation reported a united vacation church school effort with a

local Church of God congregation and described it as "a very effective ministry together," one to be repeated. Another congregation has hosted a singing group from a Church of God college.

5. Christian Church colleges and area unity gatherings have invited Church of God persons as guest leaders or visitors.

6. Eleanor Daniel, Christian Churches faculty member then at Cincinnati Bible Seminary, was invited to attend the 1991 annual meeting of the Commission on Christian Higher Education of the Church of God and offered helpful perceptions of the Commission's work.

7. In 1991 Kenneth Cable of the Christian Churches/ Churches of Christ addressed the Midwest Ministerial Assembly of the Church of God on the Open Forum process and David McCord, pastor and then president of the North American Christian Convention, was the invited observer to the 1991 General Assembly of the Church of God.[5]

8. In promotion of Barry Callen's 1992 biography on Rev. Lillie McCutcheon, *She Came Preaching*, both Standard Publishing and College Press agreed to assist Warner Press in reviewing the book, and College Press offered to highlight other books as well as help acquaint the Christian Churches with Church of God history and teachings.

9. Leroy Fulton, former president of Warner Southern College of the Church of God, was appointed to a senior administrative position at Pacific Christian College, was the first to include the Forum papers in a college library, recently presented to Pacific's faculty a lecture on "Who Is the Church of God?" and has begun through Pacific Christian College a periodic preaching clinic that includes participants from both communions.

---

[5]For a report on his observations and those of other "fraternal guests," see Barry Callen, ed., *Journeying Together*, 166-169.

10. In recent annual meetings of the North American Christian Convention, leaders of the Church of God have been invited to bring greetings, pray, and lead seminars. Included have been Leroy Fulton, Keith Huttenlocker, Barry Callen, and James Earl Massey.

11. Invited to the 1995 International Convention of the Church of God was Pastor Bob Russell of the Christian Churches. He was asked to give leadership in an all-day Vision-2-Grow session. Warner Press featured several of Russell's books for sale at the Convention and worked with Standard Publishing in delivering this service to our ministers. Then in the 1996 Convention in Anderson, Pastor Russell preached the Thursday evening sermon to a crowd of some 6,000. His assigned theme was "Christ Compels Us To Build Community!" He was exceedingly well received.

12. Barry Callen and James Massey of the Church of God have been invited to speak in chapel sessions at Emmanuel School of Religion in Johnson City, Tennessee, and Lincoln Seminary in Lincoln, Illinois. Byron Lambert of the Christian Churches/Churches of Christ has spoken in a chapel session of the Anderson University School of Theology of the Church of God.

13. A Biblical Literacy Task Force, composed of leaders from the Christian Churches/Churches of Christ and the Church of God, has met several times to attempt a mutual effort to do a Biblical literacy campaign under the theme "Read For Your Life." Included have been: (1) Church of God leaders Sherrill Hayes, Board of Christian Education, David Shultz, Warner Press, Fred Shively, Anderson University, and David Lawson, Leadership Council, (2) with Christian Churches leaders Sam Stone, Brian Clark, and Dick McKinley. The hope is to develop and publish materials for use by local congregations of both communions.

14. Sam Stone, editor of the *Christian Standard*, was present for an all-day conference led by Vision-2-Grow and Bob Russell. He was the guest of David Lawson and the Leadership Council of the Church of God.

15. Dean John Howard of Gardner College, the college of the Church of God in Canada, served for a considerable time as the interim pastor of the significant Gateway Christian Church in Edmonton, Alberta (formerly King Edward Park Church of Christ).

16. Barry Callen published three new books in 1995, *It's God's Church!* (Warner Press), *Contours of a Cause* (Anderson School of Theology), and *Sharing Heaven's Music* (Abingdon Press). Copies of the first two were given by the Leadership Council to members of the working group on doctrinal dialogue between the two groups for study and primary focus at the October 1995 discussion. The *Contours* book included numerous reflections arising from the years of the Open Forum.

The third, on preaching, included a chapter written by Fred Norris, a scholar of the Christian Churches. Dr. Callen also included an article by Byron Lambert in the Spring, 1995, issue of the *Wesleyan Theological Journal,* a journal Callen edits (Appendix G is a condensed version of this article). The article's subject, Christian experience, has been one of frequent discussion in the Open Forum dialogues. Also, compiled and edited by Callen in 1996 was *Journeying Together,* a documentary history of the corporate life of the Church of God movement (Anderson), published by the Leadership Council of the Church of God and Warner Press. It carries a section highlighting the Open Forum's history and accomplishments.

17. Dialogue members have noted and celebrated two new studies in the historical and theological heritage of the Christian Churches/Churches of Christ. One was *In Search of Christian Unity* by Henry Webb; the other was *Union in Truth* by James North.

18. In October, 1996, there was convened in Cincinnati, Ohio, a "Fellowship Gathering" sponsored jointly by the Dayspring Church of God and the Westwood Cheviot Church of Christ and hosted by the pastors of these congregations, Mitchell Burch and James Hutchison. This gathering of some fifty pastors and other ministry leaders from the two church fellowships recalled, worshiped, and explored ministry helps together. Other such gatherings are being planned.

19. This present volume, written jointly by Barry Callen and James North, one scholar from each fellowship, draws together many of the aspirations, processes, and ministry benefits realized to date because of the Open Forum and Doctrinal Dialogue process.

Select Study Papers On Christian Unity

During the years of work of the Task Force on Doctrinal Dialogue, numerous formal papers have been assigned and written for mutual instruction.[6] Among these have been several on the general topic of Christian unity. They are:

1. Bream, Harvey, "Unity Through Restoration" (April 1991).
2. Callen, Barry, "The Signs of Christian Unity in the History of the Church of God Reformation Movement" (March 1990).
3. Corts, David, "What Are the Signs of Christian Unity in the Acceptance of Others As Christians?" (March 1990).
4. Dwyer, Timothy, "Implications for Christian Unity in Acts 2:37-38" (April 1991).
5. Fife, Robert, "What Have Been Signs of Christian Unity In Our History?" (March 1990).
6. Fife, Robert, "Our Conception of Christian Unity" (May 1993).
7. Hines, Samuel, "Contemporary Possibilities for Christian Unity" (March 1990).
8. Huttenlocker, Keith, "Implications for Christian Unity from Acts 2:41-47" (April 1991).
9. Jones, Kelvin, "Of One Accord: My Vision for Christian Unity" (March 1990).
10. Jones, Kenneth, "Implications for Christian Unity in Acts 2:1-13" (April 1991).

---

[6]A complete set of all papers on all subjects is maintained by the Leadership Council of the Church of God with offices in Anderson, Indiana.

11. Kelley, W. Ray, "Implications for Christian Unity in Acts 2:1-13" (April 1991).
12. Massey, James, "Christian Unity: A Statement About Its Meaning and Expressions" (May 1993).
13. Newell, Arlo, "Unity Through Holiness" (April 1991).
14. Pearson, Sharon, "What Are the Signs of Christian Unity in the Acceptance of Others as Christians?" (March 1990).
15. Phillips, Calvin, "The Signs of Christian Unity in the Practice of the Ordinance of Christian Baptism" (March 1990).
16. Reese, Gareth, "Implications for Christian Unity in Acts 2:37-38" (April 1991).
17. Scott, Mark, "Implications for Christian Unity in Acts 2:41-47" (April 1991).
18. Shively, Kay, Response to Knofel Staton: "The Teaching in Acts 2:17-18 and Its Implications for Christian Unity" (April 1991).
19. Staton, Knofel, "The Teaching in Acts 2:17-18 and Its Implications for Christian Unity" (April 1991).
20. Taylor, Larry, "My Vision for Christian Unity" (March 1990).
21. Taylor, Myron, "The Grand Design for Christian Unity" (March 1989).

Chapter Five

DOCTRINE:
TESTING THE EVANGELICAL ALTERNATIVE

The Christian Churches/Churches of Christ and the Church of God (Anderson) both maintain a strong commitment to an "evangelical" perspective on Christian faith and life. The word "evangelical" carries a variety of meanings, some of them with negative nuances,[1] but we are using the term here to indicate a conservative view of Scripture as well as the view that one must have a personal relationship with Christ.[2] The Bible is authoritative and Christianity is more than any creedal formulation of beliefs or authorized church institutions and revered traditions. Liberalism by contrast often is understood to represent the stance that the Bible is not finally authoritative and truly normative for modern Christian faith and

---

[1]For a discussion of "evangelicalism," see Barry Callen, *Contours of a Cause: The Theological Tradition of the Church of God (Anderson)* (Anderson University School of Theology, 1995), 193ff.

[2]For instance, *The Concise Dictionary of the Christian Tradition*, edited by J.D. Douglas, Walter A. Elwell, and Peter Toon (Grand Rapids: Zondervan, 1989), 145, states: "In a general context it ["evangelical"] refers to a particular conservative Protestant form of Christianity that especially emphasizes the inspiration and authority of the Bible and the need for personal conversion to God."

practice. Both the CC/CC and the Church of God shun any viewpoint that diminishes the Bible as central for Christian faith.

Therefore, the whole dialogue between these two church traditions has been rooted in a commitment that the Scriptures are authoritative and should guide all approaches to doctrinal issues and Christian unity efforts. Religious "liberals" can carry on ecumenical dialogues with a greater sense of negotiability. Each participating denomination may reflect its own historic tradition, but if the presupposition is that such traditions are conditioned only by history and circumstances, then there is considerable flexibility when it comes to harmonizing differing views. But conservatives generally choose against this broad kind of flexibility. There is thought to be no room for negotiating what is judged to be truly divine revelation. Understanding Scriptural teaching may change, but in the final analysis changes in belief between dialoguing groups should occur only when all involved believers are convinced that the teaching perspective in question is in harmony with Scripture. This understanding of biblical boundaries is crucial and places some restrictions on "conservative" doctrinal dialogues that religious liberals do not normally worry about.

In the ongoing discussion between the CC/CC and the Church of God, difference in viewpoint has emerged in regard to several Christian doctrines and/or practices. We have mentioned some of these already—women in ministry, footwashing, frequency of participation in the Lord's supper, and certain aspects of church polity. It would be instructive and stimulating to explore each one of these differences, but the purpose of this chapter is to single out just one issue as a test case for better understanding the dynamics of conservative ecumenical dialogue.

For a variety of reasons, we have chosen the topic of Christian baptism. What are the differences of understanding between the CC/CC and the Church of God? From what source(s) have these differences arisen? How important is it that full agreement be achieved in order for Christian unity to prevail?

Baptism as a Test Case

Several reasons suggest that baptism is an appropriate test case for better understanding ecumenical dialogue among conservative Christians—and especially between the CC/CC and the Church of God. Both of these groups are committed to adult baptism by immersion, in contrast to the many groups that practice sprinkling or affusion and often extend the privilege of baptism to infants. The fact that both groups are committed to immersion automatically gives them a sense of comradeship; the majority of Christians do not practice immersion exclusively. Both the CC/CC and the Church of God are committed to the concept of a believer's church—infants and young children are not considered fit subjects of baptism because they have not yet made a personal faith commitment. Both groups are also alike in that they see baptism as something any well-meaning Christian can perform. There is no sacerdotal rite of clergy here. Ordained clergy do not have a monopoly on the right to officiate at baptisms, even though normally they are the ones who will preside.

The result is that both groups have a significant number of similarities in their respective practices of baptism—no infant baptism, immersion only, and no clerical monopoly. Even so, there is not complete agreement. It is important to emphasize that both groups are convinced that their position on baptism is the more biblical one. Both groups constantly refer to biblical texts for proof of their positions and subpoints of those positions. Both want to do what is biblically correct; they just have different understandings of what that correctness is at one or two points. Considerable time has been invested in exploring these points, seeking the reasons for the interpretive differences, and asking whether full agreement at every point is a prerequisite to full fellowship together in Christ and cooperation together in ministry.

Concern About "Baptismal Regeneration"

The CC/CC generally understands baptism as being "for the remission of sins," while the Church of God is uncomfortable with such a reference. The Church of God sees the phrase "baptism for the remission of sins" as appearing to reflect baptismal regeneration, the conviction that it is the water that saves, that salvation is in the baptismal act itself. The Church of God does not see baptism as a direct cause of salvation. It may be significant to note that, in the continuing discussions, there has been no agreed-on definition of what is meant by "baptismal regeneration." The Church of God scholars have expressed their concern that the CC/CC seems to accept baptismal regeneration. The CC/CC has vehemently denied that they do. Indeed, the phrase is used with different meanings by different people. One important lesson learned is that terminology often confuses more than clarifies intended meaning.

Jack Cottrell, a CC/CC theologian, expresses his concern over this phrase. "Strictly speaking, the idea of baptismal regeneration as taught by some church groups (especially traditional Roman Catholicism and Anglicanism) means that the proper application of baptism automatically produces regeneration even in the absence of faith on the part of the recipient."[3] Cottrell continues:

> But such "baptismal regeneration" is *not* the same as the Biblical teaching that generation occurs **during** baptism *but only when faith is also present*. It is very misleading and prejudicial to label this latter as "baptismal regeneration," especially when this term has so many negative connotations in most of Protestantism today.[4]

---

[3]Jack Cottrell, *Baptism, A Biblical Study* (Joplin, MO: College Press Publishing Company, 1989), 133, citing G.W. Bromiley, "Baptismal Regeneration," *Evangelical Dictionary of Theology*, ed. Walter A. Elwell (Grand Rapids: Baker, 1984), 119.

[4]Cottrell, *Baptism*, 133.

Church of God theologians agree fully with Cottrell when he insists that faith must be present—it surely is not the ritual of baptism that regenerates. But they question the time reference of *"during* baptism," arguing instead that baptism is to *follow* the regeneration that has occurred because of an act of faith. "Repent and be baptized" is understood to mean that regeneration (new birth) follows the act of repenting faith and then baptism follows as the new believer's act of witness, commitment, and chosen identification with God's people and mission. As Gilbert Stafford puts it: "Water baptism is the Lord's designated way for the new identity in Christ [new birth] to be declared."[5]

Obviously, then, equally serious believers in biblical teaching can and do understand somewhat differently the same biblical passages. Why is this—and how important is coming to a completely common understanding and practice? The CC/CC and Church of God movements are non-creedal in nature, meaning at least that they are very much aware of the humanness of formalized statements of Christian belief and are anxious to avoid allowing such things to become unnecessary obstacles to the unity of the body of Christ. Particular believing traditions are treasured and not quickly abandoned; but attempts are made to avoid canonizing as final and mandatory for others that which is not necessarily essential to defining the Christian faith itself.

Reaction to Individual Histories

One of the significant items learned in the continuing Dialogues on Doctrine is that each church group has been influenced by what it has reacted to in the past. The Church of God, in its continuing emphasis on needed holiness and the negative impact of humanly derived institutionalism in the church's life, has seen itself as reacting to

---

[5]Gilbert Stafford, *Theology for Disciples*, 451.

the formal, ritual sacramentalism of Roman Catholicism. As a result, its understanding of baptism involves considerable caution about anything that smacks of "works righteousness" or an automatic conveyance of saving divine grace at the hands of powerful clergy and in the contexts of mandatory and carefully controled church rituals. The tendency, therefore, is to see baptism as an opportunity for witness and celebration in obedience to a command of the Lord, but not causally related to the saving process itself.

At the second meeting of the Open Forum meetings between the CC/CC and Church of God, one Church of God scholar said that "after I had been saved for several months, I came to understand that it was important that I be baptized."[6] Similarly, at the Third Open Forum in Lexington, a woman from the Church of God mentioned in one of the small group breakouts that one winter she and her family were snowbound on the farm. During that immobility she was saved, and then she was baptized four months later. In a paper presented in 1992 Arlo F. Newell reported that he baptized his wife who "had been saved for years but had never followed the Lord in baptism due to growing up in a holiness church that did not place emphasis upon baptism."[7] Lillie McCutcheon stated that "the new birth must precede baptism."[8] All of these references agree that salvation and baptism have no necessary, immediate, or causal connection to the practice and even language of baptism.

Spencer Spaulding refers to the "fear of ceremonialism" in the Church of God movement. Religious actions which

---

[6]L. Spencer Spaulding, "What are the Signs of Christian Unity in the Practice of the Ordinance of Christian Baptism in the Church of God?" paper presented at the Open Forum, March 14, 1990, 1.

[7]Arlo F. Newell, "Seekers Together: Our Understanding of Salvation. . . . How and When Is One Saved?" paper presented at the Second Meeting of the Task Force on Doctrinal Dialogue, June 8, 1992, 10.

[8]Lillie McCutcheon, "The Ordinances of the Church of God," paper presented at the Open Forum, March 15, 1989, 4.

had no relationship to inner spiritual realities have held a peculiar horror for those in the Church of God."[9] It is this fear of ceremonialism which has led the Church of God to be especially leery of "baptismal regeneration," the belief that a person can be saved merely by yielding to any sacred ceremony. This opposition to mere ceremonialism is genuine within the Church of God, yet its theological language sometimes indicates an acceptance of certain aspects of "ceremony." McCutcheon refers to baptism as "the ceremonial induction into a new order."[10] Barry Callen states that "baptism is a ceremonial representation of the burial and resurrection of our Lord, dramatizing the believer's having followed Christ in such death and resurrection."[11] Callen also cites Charles Brown, another Church of God writer, who explained why the Church of God prefers the word "ordinance" to "sacrament." "The word sacrament implies that the ceremony in question is a channel of divine grace which works of itself with magical effect, with little or no regard to the faith or spiritual receptivity of the candidate."[12] Callen adds words from church historian John W.V. Smith in affirming the preference for "ordinance" rather than "sacrament."[13]

In this latter point the CC/CC strongly agrees. With the exception of trained theologians and other academics, the term "sacrament" is rarely heard among the CC/CC. "Ordinance" is the preferred word. But on the earlier point, the coincidence in time of acknowledging salvation and accepting baptism, CC/CC differ from the Church of God. Here again, history plays a large part. The CC/CC grew largely as a reaction to American frontier Calvinism

---

[9]Spaulding, "What are the Signs," 4.

[10]McCutcheon, "The Ordinances," 2.

[11]Barry L. Callen, "Symbols and/or Channels of God's Grace: The Status of Baptism, Communion, and Footwashing in the Theological Tradition of the Church of God Movement," paper presented to the Task Force on Doctrinal Dialogue, June, 1992, 15.

[12]Ibid., 7.

[13]Ibid.

in the early nineteenth century. The emphasis of that Calvinism was that God had predestined the elect to be saved, even if it was not always clear who the elect were. Many people on the frontier were desirous of salvation, but believed they had to await some mysterious moving of the Holy Spirit to vouchsafe to them their elect status. Some grieved for years over this agonized waiting.[14]

In reaction to this trauma, the leaders of the Stone-Campbell Movement focused on the availability of the gospel and the possibility of any individual's accepting the salvation that God has so lovingly provided. Walter Scott, pioneer evangelist in the Western Reserve of northeastern Ohio in the 1820s, developed a "five finger exercise" to explain the "plan of salvation." A person is to believe the gospel, repent of sin, and be baptized; God will grant remission of sins, and the joint gifts of the Holy Spirit and eternal life. This methodology still retains warm support among the CC/CC. They (and the Church of God) remain opposed to Calvinism with its apparently whimsical pre-destination. Together, these two groups point with assur-ance to the biblical statement, "repent and be baptized for the remission of sins." This promise of forgiveness elimi-nates the concern about whether one is elect; if one has been baptized (and this assumes, of course, proper sincer-ity and intention), God's promise holds true. That is why CC/CC generally points to baptism as the occasion of a believer's certainty of salvation.

Church of God writers generally come from a Wesleyan theological tradition and thus agree readily that God's saving grace is available to all people. However, they reg-ister some discomfort with Scott's "five finger exercise."

---

[14]Cases in point here are the biographies of Barton W. Stone and "Raccoon" John Smith. Their stories can be seen in John Rogers (ed.), *The Biography of Elder B. W. Stone, Written by Himself* (Cincinnati: J.A. & U.P. James, 1847), also available in various reprints; and John Augustus Williams, *Life of Elder John Smith* (Cincinnati: R.W. Carroll, 1870). A more popularized version of the latter is Louis Cochran, *Raccoon John Smith: A Novel Based on the Life of the Famous Pioneer Kentucky Preacher* (New York: Duell, Sloan and Pearce, 1963).

They tend to see it as too mechanical, rationalistic, and thus vulnerable to a works-orientation. Thus, while in practice the action of preaching for conversions may be quite similar in these two groups, the understanding of the process of salvation is not identical. The Church of God, reflecting its Wesleyan-holiness background, puts a greater emphasis on heartfelt experience, including the work of the Holy Spirit in granting new birth and the assurance of salvation prior to baptism, while the CC/CC has confidence that faith, repentance, and baptism, sincerely undertaken, will evoke God's promise of forgiveness and are all involved in the gaining of assurance of salvation. When the Church of God speaks about "the primacy of religious experience" prior to and justifying baptism, the CC/CC feels uncomfortable, fearing that such an emphasis is vulnerable to opening up a Pandora's box of subjective emotionalism.

The positions of these two groups, similar in most respects, do tend to reflect differing sensitivities, sensitivities that may be as historically conditioned as biblically mandated. It may be that both patterns of emphasis have legitimacy and can function to protect each other from the potential downside of existing without the other.

Nuances of Language and Meaning

The Church of God and the CC/CC also have slightly different understandings of the relationship of baptism to church membership. First of all, the Church of God focuses its thought on membership in the universal church of God, not primarily in local or denominational gatherings of believers. The CC/CC, because of its close association of baptism and the remission of sins, sees baptism as that point where one symbolically accepts Christ as Savior and thus becomes a Christian. Becoming a Christian automatically is understood to make a believer a member of the Body of Christ. Thus, membership in the church universal is assumed, as it is in the Church of God.

However, whenever this baptism takes place within the context of a local congregation of believers, the CC/CC also automatically assumes that the individual has become a "member" of that local body.

Another difference at the verbal level between these groups can be seen in a phrase that is common to much of the evangelical world, including the Church of God. Baptism is often referred to as "an outward sign of an inward grace." Except for sophisticated theologians, this phrase will only rarely be heard within the CC/CC. For many it seems to refer to a sacramental transaction which raises their rationalist, Enlightenment suspicions. It may be ironic that the Church of God sees incipient sacramentalism in the CC/CC emphasis on "baptism for the remission of sins" while itself using a phrase that strikes the CC/CC as covert sacramentalism. Such is the nature of language and the fact that different groups bring different historical baggage along with their vocabularies.

Another indication of the differing nuances of terminology is found in the use of the term "obedience" with regard to baptism. Church of God teachers, focusing on salvation being accomplished prior to participation in baptism, tend to think of baptism as a subsequent act of obedience. CC/CC ministers and theologians normally do not put such emphasis on obedience. They see the purpose of baptism as being more than obedience; it is for remission of sins and thus is a crucial aspect of the salvation process itself. While the Church of God sees the CC/CC emphasis on remission of sins as a subtle works orientation, the CC/CC sees the Church of God emphasis on obedience as a works orientation too far removed from the experience of regeneration.

Throughout these past years of the Open Forum and Dialogue on Doctrine, neither of these two church groups has expressed any wish to affirm a works righteousness or to be misunderstood as teaching "baptismal regeneration." Leaders of each group have increased in their understanding and even appreciation of the focus of the other. Full agreement has not been achieved, but this failure has not been seen as an insurmountable obstacle to true Christian unity. In fact, the process of candidly exploring doctrinal differences has only increased the self-understandings and appropriate humility of each body involved.

Although full agreement on exact wording about a Christian belief is not necessarily a sure sign of authentic Christian unity, participants in the Dialogue on Doctrine have discussed the subject of Christian baptism often. In this process they have increased considerably their mutual understanding and appreciation of each other's traditional language and nuances of meaning about baptism. It may be useful in this regard to call attention to a recent statement by theologian Clark Pinnock which articulates a perspective that both of the Dialogue groups probably could accept readily.[15] He writes:

> Baptism appears to be the occasion when the Spirit comes. There is not a dichotomy between water baptism and Spirit baptism. In the sacrament of water baptism, God blesses those who respond to his Word. More than symbol or act of obedience, the act has a spiritual effect. In baptism a person reaches out and God gives the Spirit. This does not imply that the Spirit was absent before, for clearly he was working preveniently and in the hearing of the Word. It is not so much that the Spirit is tied to water as that baptism is part of a conversion complex in which the Spirit is received. The connection is not rigid. People are converted and then seek baptism. Cornelius was dramatically converted and filled with the Spirit before water baptism (Acts 10:44-48). Nevertheless, water and Spirit baptism are associated, and an encounter with the Spirit should be expected with the sacrament.[16]

---

[15]For wording about Christian baptism that Dialogue partners have developed together and agreed on, see Appendix I.

[16]Clark H. Pinnock, *Flame of Love: A Theology of the Holy Spirit* (Downers Grove, IL: InterVarsity Press, 1996), 167.

Summary and Conclusion

After all the above has been said, some summary comments may be appropriate. It seems obvious that much of the difference between these two groups on the subject of baptism is semantic. Granted, there are different viewpoints and theological presuppositions, but one has to wonder how much of the difference is simply the continuation by more modern generations of the emphases and language of each group's pioneers based on their historical reactions to frontier Calvinism and Roman Catholicism. It may be significant that, after several years of these current discussions, in early 1996 the representatives of each group harmoniously agreed to this significant statement on baptism:

> We are agreed that baptism is commanded by the Lord Jesus to be practiced by all of His followers. This baptism is to be by the immersion in water of penitent believers. Baptism is symbolic of the atoning death, burial, and resurrection of Christ. By its nature as well as by biblical teaching, baptism is involved with forgiveness of sin. We take pains, however, to repudiate any doctrine of baptismal regeneration, holding that forgiveness is wholly a matter of God's grace.[17]

Both groups of participants in the discussions were somewhat surprised when this consensus statement emerged among them. It indicates that, despite the differences in preferred terminology and historical sensitivities that now are over a century old, both groups are close enough in spirit and practice to verbalize their biblical understandings in terms the other can readily accept. It is certain that not every one of the eighteen individuals involved (ten from the CC/CC, eight from the Church of God) was completely satisfied with every phrase in the entire consensus statement (see Appendix I). Yet the mere

---

[17]One paragraph of an eight-part consensus statement adopted by the Task Force on Doctrinal Dialogue, April 20, 1996. See Appendix I.

fact that a consensus statement could emerge at all was regarded as a wholesome and pleasing development, a work of God. It gave them confidence that there is hope for a broader range of agreement between the two fellowships on most doctrinal points. Again, however, agreement at every point is not necessarily a prequisite to experiencing the oneness for which the Lord prayed. Note this fine statement:

> In what God has revealed, let us have unity. In what He has not revealed, let us have liberty. In innovations, let us have caution not to violate another's conscience. In all things, let us have love, which means that we seek the other man's good. Let us determine to have the same head, be in the one body, led by the same Spirit, serving the same Lord, immersed into one body, giving us the same hope. Then and only then do we have any hope of seeing the same God.[18]

Where all this may go in the future is certainly not known at this point. But both groups feel the obligation, in the name of Christ and under the power of His Spirit, to continue the theological discussions. The talks have sometimes been tedious; sometimes the disagreements have been painful. But the continuing discussions have yielded the satisfying reward of broad consensus amid the developing context of mutual appreciation and acceptance.

We must again point out that this coming together has happened to two groups that have consistently expressed their loyalty to the authority of Scripture. Candid and extended discussions in which each group has invested a great deal of mental energy and time have brought forth tentative harmony and a desire to continue the process. The participants are confident that what has happened here can be a challenge to other conservative/evangelical groups. Ecumenical endeavors need not be the private preserve of the liberal denominations. A conservative paradigm may be emerging here which deserves broader notice.

---

[18]George Faull in *Christian Standard* (November 17, 1996), 10.

Chapter Six

VOICE:
JOINING THE LARGER DISCUSSION

Given the scene, challenge, goal, path, and doctrinal test case detailed in the above chapters, what now is worth saying to the larger Christian community? What has been learned in these "Open Forum" years of dialogue between the Christian Churches/Churches of Christ and the Church of God (Anderson) that is worthy of wider attention—maybe even in need of wider critique? This chapter seeks at least to begin answering such questions. The historic unity visions of these two church bodies now need to be communicated, tested, tried and refined in the larger arena of the Body of Christ. These two movements, after all, exist for the larger body and not for themselves.

No Longer on the Outside

Princeton sociologist Robert Wuthnow has shown convincingly that, at least since the 1960s, denominationalism has declined as a primary structuring factor in American Christianity.[1] This significant fact is not merely

---

[1]Robert Wuthnow, *The Restructuring of American Religion: Society and Faith Since World War II* (Princeton: Princeton University Press, 1988).

an American phenomenon and it was a trend well before the 1960s. The two movements featured in this volume, for example, ever since the nineteenth century have decried the evils typically related to denominationalism and have sought an end to the Christian community being structured (divided) in this unnatural manner. A central question for this final chapter is how best these two movements can join the larger search for workable if only partial solutions to division, rather than primarily denouncing the problem from the sidelines.

Numerous writers have characterized the twentieth as the "ecumenical century" for Christians. This characterization means at least that the negative consequences of the dividedness of Christians finally has come into focus for thousands of Christian leaders. They have represented hundreds of Christian bodies worldwide and have helped to initiate serious efforts at addressing this problem of division.

Taking seriously a unifying impulse was evidenced by one key Christian leader many generations ago. "Come, my brother," wrote John Wesley in his 1749 *Letter to a Roman Catholic*, "and let us reason together. . . . And let us resolve in all our conversation, either with or concerning each other, to use only the language of love; to speak with all softness and tenderness, with the most endearing expression which is consistent with truth and sincerity."[2] The following year his sermon *Catholic Spirit* called on all "who believe in the Lord Jesus Christ, who love God and man," to join him in a common evangelistic cause. Wesley announced that, once the vital hand of fellowship had been exchanged, he was prepared to "talk, if need be, at a more convenient season" of such matters as theological "opinions," "modes of worship," and "forms of church government."[3]

---

[2]John Wesley, "Letter to a Roman Catholic," *The Works of John Wesley*, ed. Thomas Jackson (London: Wesleyan Conference Office, 1872, reprint, Grand Rapids: Zondervan, 1958-59), 10:80-86.

[3]Sermon 39, "Catholic Spirit," in *The Works of John Wesley*, the Bicentennial Edition (Nashville: Abingdon Press, 1984—), 2:81-95.

With this heritage in mind, Albert Outler expressed the hope that modern Methodism could function beyond the normal attitudinal walls of divided Christianity. It ought to be an "evangelical order of witness and worship, discipline and nurture" within "an encompassing environment of catholicity."[4] The Christian Churches/Churches of Christ and the Church of God (Anderson) movements have been seeking a similar end for the whole of the Christian community. For many Christians, however, it has not been obvious that the initiatives of the ecumenical century have always been in the best interests of authentic Christian unity. The generous spirit of a John Wesley, while admired, is thought to open the door for theological compromising and too easy an endorsement of the denominational status quo.

As seen in chapters 1 and 2, "evangelicalism" in general and particularly conservative movements carrying a heavy burden for Christian unity (like the Christian Churches/Churches of Christ and the Church of God [Anderson])have chosen to stand apart from most ecumenical organizations. Instead, they have sought to maintain their own witness to a "more authentic" vision of unity—or in some cases have not seen the unity issue as a priority agenda item for today's church. "Restorationist" movements have sought to live from a theological ideal of what the church should be. They have championed enthusiastically the fact that the church is a spiritual reality that far exceeds sociological structures called denominations, but they have struggled with the coordinate reality that the church also is an historical reality that gets shaped by a range of non-theological forces and requires structures for practical existence.

Now the irony of standing apart for the sake of unity is quite apparent. The question is becoming less, "What are the obvious shortcomings of bodies like the World and

---

[4]Albert Outler in *The Wesleyan Theological Heritage: Essays of Albert C. Outler*, eds. Thomas C. Oden and Leicester R. Longden (Grand Rapids: Zondervan, 1991), 225f.

National Council of Churches?" It is becoming more, "What if anything do we, we who are committed to biblical revelation and oneness of the body of Christ, have to contribute to the ongoing Christian quest for unity?" Do we continue to stand outside and only complain about the inadequate visions and attempts of others, or do we join the larger conversation and seek actively to have our voice heard? Gilbert Stafford put the current challenge this way as he addressed the World Forum of the Church of God convened in Sydney, Australia, in July, 1995:

> The Church of God (Anderson) ought to be making itself available to other church groups for the purpose of asking the following question both of them and of ourselves: What changes do all of us need to make in order to be the one church which is pleasing to God? Others can see things in us which need to be changed, things which we cannot see in ourselves. They have contributions to make to us, and we have contributions to make to them which in God's spiritual economy perhaps only they can make to us and only we can make to them.[5]

Begin By Listening[6]

If the larger conversation about Christian unity is joined, it should not be joined defensively or accusingly, but constructively and hopefully. A good early strategy is to listen and learn before being tempted to make dramatic pronouncements at the expense of others.

Note was made in chapter two of guest church leader Michael Kinnamon addressing a gathering of leaders of the Christian Churches/Churches of Christ and critiquing

---

[5]See the text of this presentation in Barry Callen, ed., *Journeying Together: A Documentary History of the Corporate Life of the Church of God* (Anderson, IN: Leadership Council of the Church of God and Warner Press, 1996), 173-176.

[6]Portions of this section are dependent on Barry Callen, ed., *Journeying Together*, 166-169.

that body's relative lack of practical initiative on behalf of Christian unity. A similar critique by "outside" guest observers was invited and experienced by several sessions of the General Assembly of the Church of God meeting annually in Anderson, Indiana. One of the observers was a representative of the Christian Churches/Churches of Christ. A brief review of their observations is instructive for movements seeking a voice in the larger Christian community for the sake of Christian unity.

Between 1987 and 1994 the officers of the General Assembly took initiative to bring some ecumenical perspective to its annual meetings. They invited a series of "fraternal guests" to observe, evaluate, and then address the Assembly, with their addresses then published in the *Yearbook of the Church of God.* These guests were Clyde VanValin, Bishop of the Free Methodist Church (1987), Myron Augsburger, Mennonite college president and theologian (1988), Billy Melvin, Executive Director of the National Association of Evangelicals (1990), David McCord, pastor and president of the North American Christian Convention (1991), B. Edgar Johnson, retired General Secretary, Church of the Nazarene (1993), and Dennis Kinlaw, Old Testament scholar and past president of Asbury College (1994).[7] The following is a condensed presentation of the perspectives of these Christian leaders on the General Assembly of the Church of God, and of the movement itself.[8]

Humorously, David McCord reported that, "as one of our great American philosophers, Yogi Berra, has said,

---

[7]Robert H. Reardon, retired president of Anderson University, functioned as the fraternal guest in 1992. Being from the Church of God movement, however, portions of his comments are found elsewhere in this volume rather than here. He really functioned as an elder statesperson in his address to the 1992 Assembly.

[8]In 1995 the 32nd General Conference of the Free Methodist Church convened on the campus of Anderson University in Anderson, Indiana. Dr. Barry L. Callen was appointed by the bishops of this denomination to serve on a "Findings Committee" that functioned in a way similar to these fraternal guests to the General Assembly of the Church of God.

'You can observe a lot just by looking.'" The observation most commonly made by these fraternal guests might be described as the "enthusiastic ethos" of the Assembly. McCord, for example, reported: "I like the enthusiasm of your singing and worship. I appreciate very much the fervency of your prayers and the joyous fraternal spirit that I have discovered here." VanValin spoke of a "winsome style" by which "you celebrate easily and joyfully" with a distinctive "unity within diversity." He said that "you are an anointed people of God" who appear to feature "a trust in the integrity of each other without the need of an authoritarian hierarchy."

Myron Augsburger reported observing "the spirit of praise and joy" functioning with a "spirit of freedom and openness" and a special "sense of community." B. Edgar Johnson noted the role of music in strengthening this community. He referred to the song "O Church of God" as the movement's "national anthem." When he first heard it sung by the Assembly, "I couldn't help but feel enthused. . . . I've since had the opportunity to read the words and I enjoyed and appreciated them very, very much." Dennis Kinlaw observed that "wherever God is among his people, music develops. . . . There is within you a sense of loyalty to your tradition. . . . Pay any price to keep it, not to sanctify the past, but don't you lose those roots."

Kinlaw, however, issued an important caution along with his observation about roots. He called on the Assembly to develop further its sense of church history before Daniel Warner in the late nineteenth century. In the body of Christ "we've got four thousand years of history and if you are a part of that kingdom, all of that history at its essence belongs to you. . . . Any denomination that is less than a hundred years old is a sect by definition."

Affirmations of distinctive emphases of the Church of God movement were common in the statements of these ecumenical guests. VanValin, for example, spoke of the movement's focus on Christian unity as "a message that we all need to hear expounded and demonstrated." Augsburger characterized this unity emphasis as something "the Christian world needs to understand because it is far more biblical and far more dynamic than an organizational ecumenicity. It is an ecumenical spirit." With this affirmation, however, there also came a challenge.

VanValin put the challenge in question form: "What if you exported more frequently and fervently your message, your music, your vision of the body of Christ throughout the whole evangelical movement? We need that message and we welcome it." Billy Melvin was direct and specific: "I wonder why I have not seen more involvement by the Church of God in the community I represent—the National Association of Evangelicals. I believe with all my heart that the Church of God has something to share with those larger bodies of Christ. You have some great rootage and great fruitage in your fellowship." Beyond sharing, Melvin noted, "I believe you could also learn from this experience as you would share in the larger body of Christ."

Other affirmations clustered around the subject of "holiness." As a Mennonite, Myron Augsburger wanted to be sure that "we are not just talking about whether I smoke or drink; we are also talking about how I feel toward the poor and the dispossessed and the issue of violence." Melvin warned similarly that the world today "is not so much interested in our *talk* as our *walk*. He affirmed the longstanding emphasis of the Church of God movement on holy living, noting that "few evangelical denominations that I know have done as beautiful a job in involving our black brothers and sisters and other ethnics and minorities as you have in your [Church of God] fellowship."

A final affirmation centered around the concept of "movement" that is highlighted by the Church of God tradition. VanValin called for a retaining of this focus and pointed with admiration to the International Convention of the Church of God that convenes annually in Anderson,

Indiana—of which the General Assembly is a part. He observed: "The Convention and the Assembly, the camp meeting, this week-long annual event . . . is the glue that holds the Church of God together. You do not depend on structures and processes, form and legislation to make you who you are so much as you depend on this gathering." Added Kinlaw:

> I love the vision that brought you [Church of God movement] into existence, the one that transcends denominational lines, but, more than that, the one that champions the unity of the body of Christ. I think what promoted this was a deep sense of "seek ye first the Kingdom of God and His righteousness" in which Kingdom loyalties were put ahead of all other loyalties. You've got an organization now, but don't lose that trans-organizational vision. You must lead the way in sharing it so that the rest of us that are trapped can see somebody who cares more about the Kingdom of God than they care about their own organization. The Kingdom is first. Now, that's part of who you are.

Kinlaw warned the movement never to lose the heart of its heritage: "Don't let anything stop within you that hunger for the Spirit to work in your midst."

There were other observations and cautions in the area of the church and organization. Augsburger observed that the Church of God movement is "wrestling, as we [Mennonites] are, with what it means to be persons who have a polity of order without selling oneself out to institutionalization." Melvin openly wondered "if perhaps so much emphasis in the Church of God movement has been placed on independence of the local church that there has not been sufficient emphasis on the interdependence of the whole church. You are moving to a point in time when you are going to have to work harder with what it means to interrelate one with the other as local churches." Edgar Johnson reflected further with this advice:

> If we depend on organization for success, we may fail; but if we don't organize we may fail too. . . . There is a prob-

lem with lack of structure. It could be like a body without a skeleton, lacking direction. Probably some of your expressed fears about structure in the church's life may be carried over from a long-ago problem—maybe a problem in the thinking of the early founders of the Church of God movement that may not exist today.

Perhaps the observation and caution of Myron Augsburger serves best as a general summary. To the Assembly of 1988 he said:

You use *movement* language; I like that. Movement means something that is dynamic, something that is happening. The risen Christ is moving among us, the Holy Spirit is doing something. That also means that I (we) have to become flexible and be willing to be vulnerable— not act as though I (we) have captured the Kingdom. To date, the Church of God movement has visioned rightly and worked diligently in this regard.

For theologically conservative movements to carry meaningfully a real burden for Christian unity at the end of the twentieth century will require some careful thought and bold action. To join the larger conversation, as noted above, Christians committed to biblical authority must determine to move from the margins of the conversation and be willing to listen with care to what Christian brothers and sisters are saying about the unity and mission of Christ's body today. Then, as we explore below, it will be necessary to (1) process a central paradox, (2) recognize that the Spirit really is speaking to the churches, (3) honor the necessary limits of creedal exclusiveness, and (4) be prepared to be warmed and warming in relationships with the larger Christian community.

Facing the Paradox of Anti-Denominationalism

Joining constructively the larger unity-seeking dialogue among Christians about unity and mission will require appropriate recognition of the historical limitations of one's own movement. One of many Christian traditions that has struggled to recognize its own historical limitations is the Churches of Christ. A defining characteristic of this tradition from its beginning in the early 19th century was the intent to restore primitive Christianity. Using the words "sect" and "denomination" in their classic sociological senses, signifying social realities and not theological ideals, a current historian of this tradition speaks of it as having evolved into a denomination in the 20th century after having begun as a sect. While a typical developmental pattern, this case is said to be unusual because the Churches of Christ "have passionately rejected the labels *sect* and *denomination* as pertinent their own identity. . . . This unique self-understanding has served to create institutional identity out of a denial of institutional identity, and it has shaped the history and character of Churches of Christ in countless and often paradoxial ways."[9]

A similar paradoxical identity has been faced by the Church of God (Anderson), once referred to critically by some as the "No-Sect Sect."[10] While thoroughly committed since the nineteenth century to standing outside denominational division, this movement has evolved its own institutions and pattern of relative distinctiveness. Recently it has sought to restructure itself at the national level to better prepare for effective ministry in the 21st century. The consultant used in this process, Leith Anderson, observed the following in his final report to the movement's General Assembly(1966): "There is a very

---

[9]Richard Hughes, *Reviving the Ancient Faith: The Story of Churches of Christ in America* (Grand Rapids: Eerdmans, 1996), 2. For other examples of American church movements seeking to deny their own human histories and limitations in favor of their theological ideals, see Richard Hughes and Leonard Allen, *Illusions of Innocence* (Chicago: University of Chicago Press, 1988).

[10]Barry Callen, "The Polemics of Early Applications," which is chapter three of the masters thesis titled *Church of God Reformation Movement (Anderson, IN), A Study in Ecumenical Idealism* (Asbury Theological Seminary, 1969). In this case, the critics of the then very new Church of God movement were leaders of the Free Methodist Church.

strong desire [in the Church of God] to be described and identified as a movement and not as a denomination. However, the Church of God retains few characteristics of a movement and many characteristics of an aging denomination." Aging denominations, he said, have entrenched bureaucracies, devote resources to institutional perpetuation, and are maintained "more by past loyalty and exclusiveness than by future mission and inclusiveness."

The General Assembly received this report of "an outsider" with appreciation and determined that, to the extent these observations are true, change back in the direction of movementalism must come. Prepared anew to be appropriately self-critical, this movement appears to agree with this significant statement of Robert Fife:

> The havoc among the people of God is not caused by the mere existence of particular groups, which assume distinctive names. The havoc is wrought when a particular community of understanding or concern *invest their particularity with the dignity, authority, and identity which properly belong to the whole people of God.* This is the denomination—and this is its sin.[11]

The Roman Catholic Church has a long history of appearing to be a "denomination" attributing to itself that which belongs only to the whole people of God. Especially at Vatican Council I (1869-1870) when the doctrine of papal primacy and infallibility was established, the Catholic Church took an almost completely defensive stance, resisting aggressively what the Protestant Reformers had tried to say. Nearly another century would pass before the voices of Luther and Calvin would be given an appreciative hearing and Catholicism's institutional arrogance would be softened (Vatican Council II, 1960s). The Church of God movement (Anderson) originated and developed early in an environment highly

---

[11]Robert Fife, *Celebration of Heritage* (Los Angeles: Westwood Christian Foundation, 1992), 296. For additional material from this significant source, see Appendix E.

critical of this yet-unsoftened arrogance. Its biblical interpreters often associated the "Beast" of Revelation 13 with
the Roman Catholic Church.

Now, of course, it is crucial that movements like the
Church of God not act arrogantly in relation to its own
traditions and institutions. A recent example of intentional non-arrogance has been the formal participation of
the Missionary Board of the Church of God with "The
CoMission." This Christian mission organization has
enabled some eighty educational institutions, parachurch
groups, local churches, and mission agencies of many
denominations to recruit and train a rapid-response task
force, a Christian "Peace Corps" determined to function
together as the one Body of Christ in helping the former
Soviet Union rebuild its society on the foundation of God's
Word. All Co-Mission participants subscribe to the
Lausanne Covenant (1974), allowing a wide range of
believers to focus on the commonalities of their faith for
the sake of a major mission need and opportunity.[12]

The Spirit at Work in the Churches

According to the invitation of Revelation 2:7, "Let
anyone who has an ear listen to what the Spirit is saying
to the churches." For restoration and unity movements
like the Christian Churches/Churches of Christ and the
Church of God (Anderson), it does not come easily to even
say "churches" since this plural form of the word seems to
imply a multiplicity of what actually is singular. God has
only one church, although, of course, it does exist in a
series of local congregations like the ones first addressed
by the Book of Revelation. However, centuries of existence

[12]The mission statement of The CoMission is: "The CoMission exists for
the purpose of calling together the Body of Christ to cooperatively
share resources in order to maximize the accomplishment of the Great
Commission through forming strategic alliances and establishing
indigenous Christian Education classes for children, youth, and adults
in the 120,000 local public schools throughout the former Soviet Union
and Bulgaria, Albania, and Romania no later than December, 1997."

has brought another layer of reality to the life of the church. The church and its local congregations also now are organized into a series of historical streams of relatively distinctive traditions. Each has its special concerns about doctrine, piety, polity, and/or social issues and the church's mission.

The challenge is to see the Spirit at work in these several traditions, even the ones differing in some significant ways from one's own. The ways the traditions express their concerns may not be exactly what the Spirit is seeking to say, but listening carefully and appreciatively surely provides assistance to the Spirit's work. Says Rex Koivisto: "Differences of opinion that are honestly held can lead to profitable and fruitful discussion out of which a fuller apprehension of the truth may emerge."[13] Is it not the case that cross-denominational conversations about their respective and strongly-held views is a key to health for any church body? The intent of such conversations is not to convince the opponent Christians that they are wrong, or to decide that subjects so dear to some are really unimportant and thus a merger of the groups can happen without regard to them. Rather, a robust conversation with those who see things differently helps both groups to do their own theology better. There is value and pain, danger and gain in the process itself. As Stephen Neill has well said:

> One result of the ecumenical adventure has been a strengthening of denominational consciousness, a determination that the treasures of the denominational past shall not be jeopardized. . . . There is one thing that matters more than unity, and that is truth. A group or a Church which entered into unity at the cost of surrendering what it believed to be the truth would be committing the great treachery against light, and that means against God. If there is a conflict between unity and truth, it is truth that at all costs must be chosen. It is

---

[13]Rex Koivisto, *One Lord, One Faith: A Theology for Cross-Denominational Renewal* (Wheaton: BridgePoint, 1993), 100.

undoubtedly the case that ultimately there can be no conflict between unity and truth, since it is the God of truth who commands unity, and who commands it in order that his truth may be seen and may be believed.[14]

Humility is appropriate even in relation to the most strongly held belief statements of the various church bodies. One reason is the recognition that confessional distinctions often have arisen for more than theological reasons. Christians frequently allow themselves to be separated from each other by "secular" forces alien to the faith itself. A pioneering study has documented how churches in the United States, for instance, divided because of the roles played by class structure and slavery.[15]

Possibly the biggest hindrance to unity comes down to something quite subtle and rarely stated. It is a deep desire that one's own denominational existence be maintained. Frequently a denomination's continued existence is rationalized as necessary for the safeguarding of a particular body of inherited truth. In fact, all denominational bodies should be seen and see themselves as having life-cycles, as interim and dynamic bodies, bodies with gifts to share with the larger church, with, however, this given treasure of truth far more important than the vehicle of conveyance. All such bodies should be grateful for the treasure they carry, humble about their own long-term institutional significance to the mission of the body of Christ, and listening for the voice of the Spirit. The Spirit of God has many children, various interrelated treasures of truth, and no commitment to the supposed sacredness of any human organization devised by any group of believers.

---

[14]Stephen Neill, *The Church and Christian Union* (New York: Oxford University Press, 1968), 401. Also see James North, *Union In Truth: An Interpretive History of the Restoration Movement.*

[15]H. Richard Niebuhr, *Social Sources of Denominationalism* (1929).

Avoiding Creedal Exclusiveness[16]

If the heart of Christian identity and discipleship necessarily involves *experiencing* and then *living* the truth revealed by God in Israel and especially in Jesus Christ, then there will be strong conviction without oppressive creeds that are humanly developed and thus limited.

There was a public announcement for the Church of God camp meeting in Moundsville, West Virginia, scheduled for June, 1902. It began by saying: "A cordial invitation is given to all lovers of the truth to this general convocation of the children of God, on the campground at the Trumpet Home in the northeast part of the city." "Truth" was a central preoccupation of this community of believers. Many of this movement's adherents read closely what was being published by the Gospel Trumpet Company that was located in Moundsville at the turn of the century.[17] Surely, they believed, God has spoken and divine speech always is to be taken as prior to all other claims to wisdom. In Jesus Christ we humans have been encountered by God, and by God's fullest truth.

Often quoted among these "saints" was the New Testament verse, "Sanctify them in the truth; your word is truth" (John 17:17). This verse was not seen as a pretext for casting God's truth in another set of propositional theological statements that then could be claimed to have captured in so many words a full understanding of divine truth. Truth certainly was understood to point to objective reality; it also was judged to be personal, relational, dynamic, and contextual. Christian truth is restricted by the limits of human understanding and too often is distorted by the distracting weight of intellectualized and mandated human traditions.

---

[16]This section is heavily dependent on Barry Callen, *Contours of a Cause: The Theological Vision of the Church of God (Anderson).* Used by permission.

[17]This company is now Warner Press. It moved to its present location in Anderson, Indiana, in 1906.

117

Responding to "the truth" was believed by these sincere Christians to represent the potential of a new day for the whole church. God's light was beginning to shine again and lovers of truth were being called and privileged to "walk in the light" as God enables believers to see it. Soon these "saints" would come to sing vigorously and with joy and deep commitment:

> When the voice from heaven sounded, warning all to flee
> From the darksome courts of Babel back to Zion free;
> Glad my heart to hear the message, and I hastened to obey,
> And I'm standing *in the truth* today.[18]

One published summary of the history of the Church of God movement is titled *Truth Marches On,*[19] an appropriate way of characterizing a central burden of this movement. There has been a questing for the full truth as it is in Christ, not a crusading for any theological finality. Historian Merle Strege identifies helpfully key theological assumptions of the Church of God movement. They tend to be imbedded in the simple, yet profound phrase "lovers of truth."[20] These assumptions have much wisdom to share as followers of Christ from all traditions move into the twenty-first century. Two of these assumptions are that Christian truth is to be *experienced* and is *progressive.*

Leaders of the movement did not reduce Christianity "to a series of belief statements. . . . The real essence of Christianity was *experiencing* the truth, and that lay beyond belief." Much later than that 1902 meeting in West Virginia, the following slogan would come to be accepted widely as a brief way of identifying many congregations of this movement: "Where Christian Experience Makes You a

---

[18]"The Reformation Glory," verse 2 (emphasis added), by Charles Naylor and Andrew Byers, in *Worship the Lord* (Anderson, IN: Warner Press, 1989), 311.

[19]John Smith (Anderson, IN: Gospel Trumpet Co., 1956).

[20]See the article "Lovers of Truth" by Merle Strege in *Vital Christianity* (August 24, 1986), 22-23.

Member."[21] Such a phrase does not intend to de-emphasize the theological content of faith. The purpose is to highlight the necessity of being involved personally in radical, life-changing obedience to the call of God, the source, focus, substance, and end of all true doctrine.[22]

When the Christian faith is reduced to a matter of intellectual awareness and mechanical assent at the rational level, real understanding is compromised. To apprehend Christian faith adequately, one first must approach and embrace it with all of oneself. Then, by an enabling divine grace, one continues in the understanding process through embodying the faith in the realities of this present world. The knowing process is far more than memorized creeds. It is life and mission, believing and questing, all in constant interaction.

So the theological focus of this movement has tended to be on direct change in one's life rather than on any isolated, routinely repeated, and often arid confessional formulation of Christian faith. In fact, the usual process by which Christian communities have written and confessed formal creeds has been criticized and avoided by the movement. In part this is because the severely divided Christian community has tended to use such theological formulations in institutionally protective ways that shields many believers from real life change and significant social impact.[23] It also is because such formulations

---

[21]"A united church for a divided world" is another common self-designation of this movement, used for years on the movement's national radio broadcast in the United States and Canada, the Christian Brotherhood Hour.

[22]The Christian Churches/Churches of Christ tradition, following Alexander Campbell, has been cautious about highlighting Christian "experience." It has not shared the camp meeting tradition of the Church of God (Anderson) and is especially concerned about the potential of unchecked subjectivism in the authority structure of Christian life.

[23]"Fundamentalism" is the common term for a rigid and protective theological stance. Martin Marty says that the base theological feature of modern fundamentalisms is "oppositionalism." Their agenda is "set by what they feel or calculate demands their resistance, by what they most

often become tools to justify and maintain the dividedness of some Christians from others whose creeds or practices differ even slightly.

Church of God people seek to be clearly convictional without being narrowly and prematurely creedal. They are conservative, to be sure, but they seek to avoid being "denominationalists" in their view of the church or "fundamentalists" in their theological method. There is an appreciation for process and a disposition to be committed to the whole of truth that lies beyond the apprehension of any one tradition within the Christian community. Thus, "catholic" is an important addition to any "free church" designation of this movement.[24]

Pioneer leaders of the Church of God movement recognized that truth, beyond needing to be *experienced*, tends to be *progressive*. New light had begun to shine on the gathered darkness of church life and surely there yet would be "more light." All such light had been and always would be thoroughly biblical in its substance, but human understanding of it inevitably is partial and always should be growing. While there is only one biblical revelation on which the faith is founded, that revelation grows on us and we in it. In this sense, it is progressive (not that it evolves, changes, and is added to over time).

---

contend against" (in Hans Küng, Jürgen Moltmann, eds., *Fundamentalism As An Ecumenical Challenge*, London: SCM Press, 1992, 3). Today that target is "modernism" in its many forms. An irony is that the rationalism of modernism (the Enlightenment influence) is used extensively by Christian fundamentalists in their vigorous defense of the truth as they see it. The current fundamentalistic phenonemon is not limited to Christianity, but also is seen in Judaism and Islam, e.g. Note the multi-volume study underway by Martin Marty and R. Scott Appleby (vol. 1 is *Fundamentalists Observed*, Chicago, 1991).

[24]These descriptive phrases, while fairly descriptive of the movement's aspirations, were rarely used by the movement of itself. At first there was little focus on church history other than as the arena of apostasy. Thus the "free-church" tradition as such was little known prior to the work of Charles Brown in the 1940s and 1950s. Since Roman Catholicism was viewed as a prime example of falsely institutionalizing the church by human hands, the word "catholic" understandably has been avoided as a primary movement self-description.

The essential relationship of Christian experience, the process of knowing truth, and the related stance of openness to "new light" should not be misunderstood. These commitments are not intended to encourage movement leaders to be rash and individualistic, stepping outside the mainstream of Christian faith by exhibiting theological novelty in their thinking, believing, or acting. No one has sought or claimed any new divine revelation that surpasses what is available to all Christians or is not wholly consistent with traditional, "orthodox" thought. No "prophet" has received revelation from God that in any way has added to the substance of the Story found in biblical revelation. The task is to reform in light of the enduring biblical truth, not to extend and change that truth. This movement "is not committed to ecclesiastical standards or doctrines repugnant to human reason. We do not believe in extremism or fanaticism of any kind. We have no sympathy for strange or freak doctrines that are maintained only with subtle arguments or with forced and unnatural interpretations of Scripture."[25] There is no rash novelty, only commitment to taking seriously what is authentic, enduring, and essential to Christian life and mission.

How does the authentic, enduring, and essential become known? Jesus is reported to have called God's Spirit "the Spirit of truth" (John 14:17; 15:26; 16:13). The Spirit of God is linked closely by the New Testament record with the truth of what was being accomplished in the life of Jesus. Jesus is inseparable from the Spirit who communicates truth, especially the truth that is in Jesus himself. Those who worship the Father are instructed to do so "in spirit and truth" (4:23-24)—and Jesus is "the truth" (14:6), the truth conveyed to us by the Spirit.

The real challenge, movement leaders have insisted for generations, is to walk constantly in the light as God gives

---

[25] F.G. Smith, *Brief Sketch of the Origin, Growth, and Distinctive Doctrines of the Church of God Reformation Movement* (Anderson, IN: Gospel Trumpet Co., 1927).

121

light, not ever canonizing the spot on which one stands or institutionalizing the perception one may hold at any given time. Faith always is a pilgrimage, a journey guided by the Spirit toward more and more light. These hymn lyrics express well this humble journey:

> We limit not the truth of God, to our poor reach of mind,
> By notions of our day and sect, crude, partial, and confined.
> No, let a new and better hope, within our hearts be stirred:
> The Lord hath yet more light and truth, to break forth from the Word.[26]

Faith's focus should be on a Person more than on any proposition, even one respectfully drafted about that Person. Jesus Christ is himself the truth (John 14:6). Advice was given to Timothy so that he might be able to "fight the good fight, having faith and a good conscience (1 Tim. 1:18-19). It was made clear that God's intent is that everyone "come to the knowledge of the truth" (2:4). How is that truth identified? It centers in the belief that "there is one God; there is also one mediator between God and humankind, Christ Jesus" (2:5).

With Christ as central and the biblical revelation as the normative source for understanding Christ, the Christian life is a humble walking together as a maturing community of faith, always being shaped by the Christ Story, in the midst of searching, sharing, and living the Story. Believers are to be open to each other, resources to each other, continuing to think and experience, always inspired by the Spirit who is the conveyor of the divine light of Christ. Never without guiding, truth-full convictions, Christ's disciples also should never be without a large sail unfurled to capture any new breeze of God's ever unfolding truth.

---

[26]Verse one and refrain of "We Limit Not the Truth of God," words by George Rawson (1807-1889), based on parting words of Pastor John Robinson to the Pilgrim Fathers, 1620.

Theological conviction always should be accompanied by an appropriate humility. The direction is clear. The foundation is clear. The biblically narrated revelation is set. The Person is known. The future is open, full of challenge, both on a sure path and in process toward our fuller understanding and increasing participation in the unfolding will of God. One day, it is promised, we will see the fullness of truth itself (1 Cor. 13:12).

The early Church of God "saints" were a theologically paradoxical people, at once clearly committed, yet deliberately dynamic about any final formulations of the faith. Balance, clarity, and doctrinal fullness are not necessarily to be seen in any one of the movement's respected teachers and writers in a given generation.[27] The instinct for integrity and wholeness and the persistent "movement" openness are group aspirations believed essential to the increasing understanding of the fullness of truth over time. Here is a whole-church vision, not a closed-group operation. It is the championing of a process of joyful discovery rather than an establishment approach to theological questions.

Early movement theologian Russell Byrum (1889-1980) writes about the qualities of mind needed for a competent Christian theologian. One quality identified is a love for truth. Explains Byrum:

> Love for truth will keep one from opposite extremes of conservatism and progress. Extreme conservatism makes much of the "old paths" whether they are right or not, and persistently holds to the way which it happens to be even though the Spirit of God is endeavoring to lead into a rich and deeper spiritual life than that yet attained. . . . But proper love for truth will lead one to seek for greater

---

[27]This is not to say that at times there have not been attempts within the movement to codify and control "accepted" Christian doctrine. Once there even was a failed attempt to have judged as "standard literature" of the movement certain materials published prior to a given year in the 1920s, thus avoiding widespread acceptance of certain new ideas not acceptable to certain leaders.

light and at the same time cause him to hold fast all he has received that is really truth.[28]

The prevailing judgment of leaders of the Church of God movement is that attempts to standardize Christian truth in formal and final definitions binds to some degree the work of the Holy Spirit, retards in important ways the emerging of the fuller truth, and thus artificially stagnates the life of God's people. It is believed that God has and will continue to take the initiative in making truth known. No organizational pattern or restrictive creedal statement, no human desire or activity should be accepted if its impact is to impede the free flow of God's creating, organizing, informing, and commissioning of the church, the body of all God's redeemed. In short, Daniel Warner maintained that he had simply discovered a central spiritual principle, "the identification of the visible and invisible church in a spiritual congregation of Christians from which no Christian was excluded by any man-made rules or corporate forms of organization."[29]

Here are believers with a conviction that they (and all Christians) are to represent on a worldwide scale the modern restoration of apostolic faith, fellowship, and mission. Their longing is to return to the essence, purity, and power of New Testament Christianity. They declare themselves prepared to cast aside completely the web of theological compromise and the tangle of churchly debris that has accumulated over the centuries. Apostasy brought to the body of Christ quite the opposite of holiness and unity. The time of apostasy now should end for the sake of the church's mission.

---

[28]Russell Byrum, *Christian Theology*, rev. ed. (Anderson, IN: Warner Press, 1925, 1982), 13-14.

[29]Wrote Warner in his personal Journal (March 7, 1878): "On the 31st of last January the Lord showed me that holiness could never prosper upon sectarian soil encumbered by human creeds and party names, and he gave me a new commission to join holiness and all truth together and build up the apostolic church of the living God. Praise his name! I will obey him."

124

For too long and for far too many people there has been a usurping of the roles belonging only to God. Beginning in the 1880s, movement pioneers rejoiced that a "new day was sweetly dawning." To what Christ had defined and commanded these saints would be true. To the biblical foundation they would add nothing; from it they would drop nothing. This movement wishes to be identified with no special doctrine. Instead, as Albert Gray says, "it seeks to unite all truth held by Christians and to ascribe to each the degree of prominence given it in the Bible." The Church of God movement "does not claim to be the originator nor sole custodian of the truths that it holds, but accepts light as it is revealed and stands committed to the full truth."[30]

Warmed and Warming[31]

Unity is intended by God to be a crucial mark of the church. Division confuses, weakens, alienates, and thereby hampers mission. Where unity is understood as a dynasty of successor male bishops (apostolic succession), it is oppressive and strangles appropriate diversity and plurality. On the other hand, ecumenism, the quest for the realization of Christian unity, contrasts with the competitive mentality seen commonly in human societies. Accordingly:

> Ecumenism is a way of looking at reality that refuses to absolutize relative perspectives. It is an approach to knowledge which insists that truth is seldom discovered in isolation but rather through dialogue in diverse community. It is a way of living that dares to think globally and live trustfully with differences in community, not as a

---

[30]Albert Gray, "Distinctive Features of the Present Movement," *Gospel Trumpet* (February 23, 1922), 5.

[31]This section is heavily dependent on Barry Callen, *Contours of a Cause: The Theological Vision of the Church of God Movement (Anderson)* (Anderson University School of Theology, 1995), 158-168. Used by permission.

result of polite tolerance but on the basis of our common commitment to and experience of the creating, redeeming, and sustaining God.[32]

While Christian unity is a gift from God through the Spirit, it is realized only as Christians intentionally open themselves to be in community with other believers.[33] "Unity is given," according to James Earl Massey, "but our experience of it must be gained." The givenness roots in the fact that "the church is the community of those who honor Jesus Christ, sharing his life, teachings, and work. Belonging to him makes every believer belong to all other believers."[34] But what of the persistent dividedness among Christ's people? Believers typically experience the fellowship of God's people in connection with some denominational body. Is this fact division by definition? There appears to exist a perplexing paradox: the multiplicity of

---

[32]Michael Kinnamon, *Truth and Community*, 109.

[33]What constitutes true and viable Christian unity? Must there be full agreement on beliefs, or a single organizational network, or is the goal more in the area of attitudes? Early leaders of the Church of God movement envisioned denominational structures collapsing (not merging). For the most part that has not happened. Consideration now should be given to this judgment of Emil Brunner: "Certain as is the fact that a number of competing churches represents a scandal, equally certain is it on the other hand that a variety of forms of Christian fellowship is a necessity. . . . Far more important than organizational reunion of the historical churches is the readiness of individual Christians . . . to cooperate in a spirit of brotherliness" (*The Misunderstanding of the Church*, Philadelphia: Westminster Press, 1953, 112).

[34]James Massey, *Concerning Christian Unity* (Anderson, IN: Warner Press, 1979), 8, 11, 20. Clark Williamson adds that "unity in the church, fragmentarily but really, is where the diverse members of the body of Christ are aware of and appreciate their essential relatedness to each other, where they love one another with the kind of love with which they have been loved" (*A Guest in the House of Israel*, Louisville: Westminster/John Knox Press, 1993, 262). James Evans, Jr., says that "the solidarity of that community (koinonia of the church) . . . is strong enough to render all other stratifications among human beings of only secondary importance. Thus in the holy community 'there is no Greek nor Jew, slave nor free, male nor female'" (*We Have Been Believers: An African-American Systematic Theology*, Minneapolis: Augsburg Fortress, 1992, 136).

Christian traditions is due in part to human sin (Gal. 5:19-21) and in part to the inevitable varieties of human cultures, symbol systems, and historical circumstances that are not sinful in themselves.

We have to face the question: "How may a people who exist as a distinct community within the Church, for the sake of witness unto the unity of the Church, avoid the negation of their witness by their very existence?"[35] To avoid just such a negation, in 1804 there was published *The Last Will and Testament of the Springfield Presbytery* to explain why a reforming Christian group would dissolve its own interim "church" body, would "die the death" organizationally as a witness to Christian unity. "We will," it boldly announced, "that this body die, be dissolved, and sink into union with the Body of Christ at large; for there is but one Body and one Spirit, even as we are called in one hope of our calling."[36]

Can an identifiable Christian body successfully "sink" into the whole of God's people as a unity witness without disappearing and thus forfeiting any real base from which to witness to and help realize Christian unity? Is the divisiveness of our denominationalized Christian community so assumed and entrenched, so sociologically inevitable, that there is no alternative? Because of the hurtfulness of division to the church's mission and because the New Testament witness highlights the goal of Christian unity, even presents it as the personal prayer of Jesus on behalf of all his disciples in all times (John 17), many Christians over the centuries have affirmed that there must be an alternative to rampant division.[37] A movement that serves

---

[35]Robert Fife, "The Neglected Alternative" in *Celebration of Heritage*, 265.

[36]This document, written by Barton W. Stone, is a classic in the "Restorationist" movement.

[37]Theodore Jennings insists that "division is a problem for the identity of the church. Division is a sign of the power of the world and sin. Division is then the antisign (the countersign) to the reign of God" (*Loyalty To God*, Nashville: Abingdon Press, 1992, 188).

to upbuild the church, not divide and tear down, may be seen as a gift of the Spirit to the church.

For the Kentucky Christians led by Barton Stone and his colleagues, *The Last Will and Testament* declared an intentional "sinking" by no longer defining Christian fellowship in terms of a particular institution to which all Christians could not belong. These visionary reformers sought to become a microcosm of the whole church, with no other criteria of unity except those which can be the bond of unity for the whole church. There would be no restrictive creed mandated on all members. Evangelizing should be done *as the church* (the whole body of Christ) and for the church. Baptizing would be into the church, not into a given segment of it. The invitation to the Lord's Supper would be issued as representatives of the whole body to any in the body wishing to participate (it is, after all, the Lord's table, not ours).

How, then, should one describe groupings of Christians that seek to represent and serve the whole church in distinctive ways, without claiming for themselves those characteristics belonging only to the whole body? One helpful distinction is that between the church and "movements" within it. Affirming that the church is one and that such oneness is obscured when denominations divide the church into "churches," Robert Fife defines a "movement" as "a community of understanding and concern which exists and serves within the Church, and for its edification."[38]

Sometimes particular groupings of Christians come into being because their members share certain understandings and concerns about the faith.[39] Such distinctive

---

[38]Robert Fife, *Celebration of Heritage*, 276.

[39]Even within the New Testament we already see early approaches to understanding a unity in plurality within the church (diversity of spiritual gifts, the Christian conscience and "gray areas," cultural diversity implied in the reality of multiple congregations, their differing settings and range of approaches to problems). In each case, unity left room for some diversity. See Rex Koivisto, *One Lord, One Faith*, 37-42.

communities *within* the church (not *as* the church) help facilitate the internal dialogue of the church as the whole body seeks its maturity and unity for the sake of its mission.[40] Movements, therefore, are "characteristic of the church as a living organism." They are actions of the body of Christ rather than separations from or usurpations of the body. While a properly motivated renewal movement is not the church and seeks to keep that very clear, it is a vital part of the church and functions in order to make the church more whole and more effectual.[41]

Much like the restorationist movement represented by Robert Fife, the Church of God movement has been sensitive to the damage done to the church and its mission by denominational divisions when such divisions take to themselves the prerogatives belonging only to the whole body. It has thought of itself as a "movement" in Fife's terms, functioning at God's call *within* the body and *for* the body. Too often, however, even this unity movement

---

[40]Robert Fife, *Celebration of Heritage*, 265-271. Fife calls for denominations to cease calling themselves "churches" and assuming for themselves the dignity and prerogatives belonging only to the church (274). In this regard, note C.C. Morrison, editor of the *Christian Century*, 77:10 (March 9, 1960), 281.

[41]Rex Koivisto attributes such wholesome characteristics to "denominations" (*One Lord, One Faith*, 102ff). Such groupings, he says, are inevitable sociologically. Even people uniting around a non-denominational platform are not thereby kept from potentially being at least part of what they oppose (102). Koivisto quotes Wolfhart Pannenberg: "The mutual relationship of the various regional or denominational traditions within the one Christian world should be thought of in terms of that type of multiplicity of concrete forms in which the catholic fullness of the church comes to expression. The multiplicity of such traditions in church order, doctrine, and liturgy does not exclude catholicity as long as each of them holds itself open, beyond its own distinctive features, for the Christian rights of the others and feels a responsibility, not just for its own tradition, but for the whole of Christian history and its heritage" (104). Similarly: "A monolithic denomination is not desirable. In Christian history, revival times have often occasioned a new order in Roman Catholicism or a new denomination in Protestantism—not mergers. . . . The Church can be one and apostolic and catholic right while it exists in denominational forms" (J. Kenneth Grider, *A Wesleyan-Holiness Theology*, 484-485).

has managed to facilitate awkward separations, in spite of itself.

A movement can facilitate the internal dialogue of the church only as it engages actively with the church, not when it retreats within its own confines out of self-preoccupation or fear of contamination by the beliefs and practices of other Christian traditions. A "movement" can destroy its own genius by failing to move creatively within the larger body. Lutheranism, for instance, has sought to avoid this trap by thinking of its own confessions of faith as an offer made to the larger church.[42] When, however, an offer moves to ultimatum, lacking appreciation for the valid offers of others, a movement becomes a "sect" in the negative sense.

Denominated bodies can be honorable and effective if they are not honored as ends in themselves, if they function cooperatively as patterns of partnership in relation to the whole body, and if they function as "movements" seeking to facilitate the health of the whole church. There is nothing inherently divisive in a group of Christians following the natural sociological process of "denominating" itself. In fact,

> no one form should be judged divisive just because it is a form. . . . Diversity is not division when the spirit of relating to those beyond the group is kept alive. . . . Diversity is one thing, while a *spirit* of division is quite another. . . . Every Christian has a legacy in every other Christian. We experience that legacy only as we receive each other and relate, moving eagerly beyond group boundaries.[43]

---

[42]See E. Gritsch, R. Jenson, *Lutheranism: The Theological Movement and Its Confessional Writings* (Philadelphia: Fortress Press, 1976), chapter one. Carl Braaten speaks of Lutheranism much as the Church of God movement always has spoken of itself: "Lutheranism is not essentially a church but a movement. . . . It is a confessional movement that exists for the sake of reforming the whole church of Christ by the canon of the gospel. The . . . structures of Lutheranism are interim measures, ready to go out of business as soon as their provisional aims are realized" (*Principles of Lutheran Theology*, Philadelphia: Fortress Press, 1983, 46).

[43]James Massey, *Concerning Christian Unity*, 75, 78, 82.

A helpful analogy was shared at the centennial consultation on the heritage of the Church of God movement.[44] The Gulf Stream is a marvelous movement of water that leaves the Gulf of Mexico and flows as a warming river across the vast expanse of the Atlantic Ocean to the European continent. The general path of the warmer water is obvious. Its influence on the ocean environment is definite as it moves along. But its boundaries are imprecise. It is open to all the surrounding ocean, influencing and being influenced. T. Franklin Miller judged this an appropriate image of what a movement should be like within the larger body of Christ. The opposite, by whatever name, tries delivering its water to Europe in a sealed pipeline, neither warming nor being enriched by the much larger body on the way. The opposite of a movement (an isolated "sect") thinks it knows itself to be the true water without need of enrichment and not wishing to risk being chilled by outside contact.

Christian unity is both a gift of God and the achievement of those committed to its fullest realization. Diversity can be a source of freedom and creativity in the church, the opposite of a regimented and premature uniformity. The diamond of Christian truth has many facets. Difference is not bad unless it hardens into an arrogant, anti-catholic exclusiveness, or deviates from the biblical revelation that is to form the church in all of its expressions. Groupings of Christians need not represent an evil just because they exist as distinct groupings. The question is whether they are in conflict or communion, whether they are contributing to or detracting from the whole body of Christ. Bodies that cut themselves off are acting

---

[44]Convened in February, 1980, at the School of Theology of Anderson University, Anderson, Indiana. Note also the centennial celebration of the Church of God movement in Germany that occurred in Hamburg, Germany, September, 1994. A featured guest speaker was the director of the German Evangelical Alliance, an interdenominational Christian organization with which the Church of God movement in Germany had recently affiliated. Such affiliation expressed the desire to cooperate with, contribute to, and benefit from the larger church.

against the church, even if their divisive platforms include the call for Christian unity (an accusation sometimes leveled at the Church of God movement, particularly in its earliest decades).[45]

The church today is faced with a twin danger. Divisiveness, always tempting, is sinful in its unjustified pride and imperialism. Syncretism, however, often seeks to correct such narrowness by being willing "to do almost anything to gain an external unity" and in the process "is susceptible to mating with any ideological partner around, usually at the cost of loss of centered orthodoxy."[46] The challenge is to be orthodox and radical, belonging to the mainstream of the Christian tradition, but in a distinctive, constructive, and renewing way.

Gabriel Fackre identifies two ideological partners, new "tribes" that sometimes function today like the old sects in a negative, cut-off way. One is an "imperial tribalism" that rallies around the modernist assumption that truth comes by right knowledge and exists to make this world more livable. Since knowledge is thought to root in historical circumstance and vested interest, it is said that one knows true Christian identity only when one acts on behalf of the

---

[45]In one sense the church is called to be "sectarian." When it is the eschatological church born of the Pentecostal vision, carrying the distinctive marks, and exercising the distinctive gifts of the Spirit, the church moves toward the "sect" type of ecclesiology described by Troeltsch (*The Social Teaching of the Christian Churches*, 1912). He describes Christianity as having three organizational orientations, church, sect, and mysticism. Books like S. Hauerwas and W. Willimon, *Resident Aliens* (Nashville: Abingdon, 1989) and the whole Believers' Church tradition call for a distinctive, counter-cultural identity as the authentic way of really being the church in our kind of world. In another sense, however, the church should resist sectarianism. "The Disciples of Christ and the Church of God (Anderson, Indiana) have witnessed long and loud about the need to heal the divisions within Christendom, advising that rules and opinions not found in Scripture are injurious to fellowship and the experience of unity. The intent has been to help the rest of the churches become aware of how denominational separatism limits fellowship and hinders having a visible unity" (James Massey, *Concerning Christian Unity*, 90).

[46]Thomas Oden, *Life in the Spirit* (San Francisco: Harper, 1992), 313.

oppressed. The *doer* is the *knower*. Truth is tribally defined
since it is restricted to those involved in the prescribed way.

The other is "confessional tribalism" that knows no
final truth, "only illusory claims and interest-laden agendas ripe for deconstruction." In this instance it is assumed
that one "can never find 'the truth'; one must be content
with what one has, not things truthful but things meaningful." Our tribe is *our* tribe with our distinctive language, lore, and codes. While live-and-let-live is the
attitude, there is "border control" that maintains meaningful identity. These two tribal ideologies both threaten a
unified church, one by arrogance, the other by apathy.[47]

Organizational variety in the church appears
inevitable as Christians of varying backgrounds focus
their lives around differing concerns in order to advance
varying understandings of the gospel in multiple cultures.
The problem is not the variety as such, but rigid spirits of
exclusiveness that act *against* and not *with* and *for* the
whole church. The problem of division is its unjustified
exclusivism (a sign to the world that is injurious to
Christ's mission). Ignoring the necessary mark of catholicity, a divisive body falsely expands some insight, gift, or
group tradition into a restricting dominance, failing to
hear that "the eye cannot say to the hand, 'I have no need
of you.' . . . If the whole body were an eye, where would the
hearing be?" (1 Cor. 12:21, 17). True division makes
human experience normative, even when insisting on
scriptural authority, since only the official and humanly
conditioned reading of the particular "tribe" is judged
acceptable by that tribe.

The goal of Christian unity, possible in the midst of
diversity by the work of the one Spirit, is commitment to
the one Lord who is head of the one church. Such Christ-
centered unity is not a matter of creedal uniformity, but
consists of communication between Christian groups, the
mutual enrichment by varying traditions, with the standard

[47]Gabriel Fackre, *Ecumenical Faith in Evangelical Perspective* (Grand
Rapids: Eerdmans, 1993), 74-76, 85.

of the faith, Jesus Christ, the exclusive possession of no one group. "The fullness of the gospel proclaimed in the church," concludes Fackre, "will be in direct proportion to the mutual correction and completion of the church's tribal monologues. Let the imperialist who raids and the confessionalist who patrols dismantle their juggernauts and take down their barricades."[48]

The hope is not for a uniformity with all distinctives somehow eliminated. Christians are to be reconciled *in their diversity*. Observing that real differences already existed even in the early church, Thomas Oden insists that "genuine unity in the whole body of Christ is not merely a matter of improved organizational management. It is a unity enabled by the Spirit that awakens legitimate diversity without imposing premature uniformity."[49] Being together in Christ by the Spirit is to be "catholic." Being in touch with one's own traditional distinctives within the Christian family, while remaining open to the wisdom resident in the larger reality of the church, is to be "radical" in a divinely-intended sense. The Church of God movement has hoped in this way to be "free-church catholic," a healing and uniting force within the whole body of Christ.

There is to be a careful juxtaposition of unity and diversity, both kept focused and constructive by a divine enablement that incites the wakefulness of Christians and resists efforts at human domestication of others or of God's work. John Frame joins the tradition of the Church of God movement in calling for "ecclesiastical revolutionaries," Christians willing to yield themselves and their status-quo tribal instincts for the sake of the higher calling of God to the church.[50]

---

[48]Ibid, 86. Down should come all denominational chauvinisms that promote the interests of one Christian body over against and at the expense of others. The concern always should be for the health of the whole.

[49]Thomas Oden, *Life in the Spirit*, 311.

[50]John Frame, *Evangelical Reunion: Denominations and the One Body of Christ* (Grand Rapids: Baker, 1991), 16.

Conclusion

On judgment day, God will not ask us what sort of church *we lived in,* but what sort of church *we longed for.* Carl Braaten once put well the proper vision of the church of God's intent, the one for which we still should long:

> . . . we long for a Church which will be both evangelical and catholic, continuous with the faith of the apostles, and coterminous with all that is universally valid in the experience of Christ's body on earth. We long for a Church which will be unified and in which the one bread and the one cup may be shared by all, without regard to class, race, or denomination. We long for a Church in which all the members will be one with Christ and one with one another, even as the Son is one with the Father and the Spirit is one with both. We long for a Church which will be one and catholic, so that the mission of Christ through his Church to all the nations might be accomplished; for unity and mission belong together. The Church we long for, let us work for. God will accomplish his will, indeed, without our help, but we pray that he may accomplish it even through us.[51]

To better realize in our time the church that Christ intends has been the historic burden of both the Christian Churches/Churches of Christ and the Church of God (Anderson). The Open Forum dialogue between them, and now this resulting book, have intended to further this process under the lordship of the Christ and by the power of Christ's Spirit. May it be so, increasingly, and in ever wider circles of believers, for the sake of the mission of the church in our time.

---

[51]Carl Braaten, "Rome, Reformation, and Reunion," *Una Sancta* 23:2 (1967), 6.

Appendix A

EXCERPTS FROM THE
DECLARATION AND ADDRESS[1]
by
Thomas Campbell, 1809

Dearly Beloved Brethren:

That it is the grand design and native tendency of our holy religion to reconcile and unite men to God, and to each other, in truth and love, to the glory of God, and their own present and eternal good, will not, we presume, be denied, by any of the genuine subjects of Christianity. The nativity of its Divine author was announced from heaven, by a host of angels, with high acclamations of "Glory to God in the highest, and on earth peace and good-will toward men." The whole tenor of that Divine book which contains its institutes, in all its gracious declarations, precepts, ordinances, and holy examples, most expressively and powerfully inculcates this. In so far, then, as this holy

---

[1] Thomas Campbell, *Declaration and Address*, reprinted in *Historical Documents Advocating Christian Union*, edited by Charles A. Young, pp. 79-117. Campbell is considered one of the founding fathers of the Restoration Movement, which now is represented in part by the Christian Churches/Churches of Christ. When he left the Seceder Presbyterians in 1808 out of disgust for their sectarian pettiness, he gathered a group of followers and wrote out some principles by which he believed Christian unity could be attained. This 1809 document, the *Declaration and Address*, included thirteen propositions which contain his most significant ideas.

unity and unanimity in faith and love is attained, just in the same degree is the glory of God and the happiness of men promoted and secured. Impressed with those sentiments, and, at the same time, grievously affected with those sad divisions which have so awfully interfered with the benign and gracious intention of our holy religion, by exciting its professed subjects to bite and devour one another, we cannot suppose ourselves justifiable in withholding the mite of our sincere and humble endeavors to heal and remove them. . . .

Dearly beloved brethren, why should we deem it a thing incredible that the Church of Christ, in this highly favored country, should resume that original unity, peace, and purity which belong to its constitution, and constitute its glory? Or, is there anything that can be justly deemed necessary for this desirable purpose, both to conform to the model and adopt the practice of the primitive Church, expressly exhibited in the New Testament? Whatever alterations this might produce in any or in all of the Churches, should, we think, neither be deemed inadmissible nor ineligible. Surely such alteration would be every way for the better, and not for the worse, unless we should suppose the divinely inspired rule to be faulty, or defective. Were we, then, in our Church constitution and managements, to exhibit a complete conformity to the apostolic Church, would we not be, in that respect, as perfect as Christ intended we should be? And should not this suffice us?

It is, to us, a pleasing consideration that all the Churches of Christ which mutually acknowledge each other as such, are not only agreed in the great doctrines of faith and holiness, but are also materially agreed as to the positive ordinances of the Gospel institution. So that our differences, at most, are about the things in which the kingdom of God does not consist, that is, about matters of private opinion or human invention. What a pity that the kingdom of God should be divided about such things! Who, then, would not be the first among us to give up human inventions in the

worship of God, and to cease from imposing his private
opinions upon his brethren, that our breaches might *thus*
be healed? Who would not willingly conform to the original pattern laid down in the New Testament, for *this*
happy purpose? Our dear brethren of all denominations
will please to consider that we have our educational preju-
dices and particular customs to struggle against as well as
they. But this we do sincerely declare, that there is nothing we have hitherto received as matter of faith or practice, which is not expressly taught and enjoined in the
word of God, either in express terms or approved precedent, that we would not heartily relinquish, so that we
might return to the original constitutional unity of the
Christian Church; and in this happy unity, enjoy full communion with all our brethren in peace and charity. The
like dutiful condescension we candidly expect of all that
are seriously impressed with a sense of the duty they owe
to God, to each other, and to their perishing brethren of
mankind. To this we call, we invite, our dear brethren of
all denominations, by all the sacred motives which we
have avouched as the impulsive reasons of our thus
addressing them.

You are all, dear brethren, equally included as the
objects of our esteem and love. With you all we desire to
unite in the bonds of an entire Christian unity—Christ
alone being the head, the center, his word the rule; an
explicit belief of, and manifest conformity to it, in all
things—the terms. More than this, you will not require of
us; and less we cannot require of you; nor, indeed, can you
reasonably suppose any would desire it, for what good
purpose would it serve? We dare neither assume nor pro-
pose the trite, indefinite distinction between essentials
and non-essentials, in matters of revealed truth and duty;
firmly persuaded, that, whatever may be their compara-
tive importance, simply considered, the high obligation of
the Divine authority revealing, or enjoining them, renders
the belief or performance of them absolutely essential to
us, in so far as we know them. And to be ignorant of any-

thing God has revealed can neither be our duty nor our privilege. We humbly presume, then, dear brethren, you will have no relevant objection to meet us upon this ground. And, we again beseech you, let it be known that it is the invitation of but few; by your accession we shall be many; and whether few, or many, in the first instance, it is all one with respect to the event which must ultimately await the full information and hearty concurrence of all. Besides, whatever is done, must begin, some time, some where; and no matter where, nor by whom, if the Lord puts his hand to the work, it must surely prosper. And has he not been graciously pleased, upon many signal occasions, to bring to pass the greatest events from very small beginnings, and even by means the most unlikely! Duty then is ours; but events belong to God.

We hope, then, what we urge will neither be deemed an unreasonable nor an unseasonable undertaking. Why should it be thought unreasonable? Can any time be assigned, while things continue as they are, that would prove more favourable for such an attempt, or what could be supposed to make it so? Might it be the approximation of parties to a greater nearness, in point of public profession and similarity of customs? Or might it be expected from a gradual decline of bigotry? As to the former, it is a well-known fact that where the difference is least, the opposition is always managed with a degree of vehemence inversely propositioned to the merits of the cause. With respect to the latter, though, we are happy to say, that in some cases and places, and, we hope, universally, bigotry is upon the decline; yet we are not warranted, either by the past or present, to act upon that supposition. We have, as yet, by this means seen no such effect produced; nor indeed could we reasonably expect it; for there will always be multitudes of weak persons in the Church, and these are generally the most subject to bigotry; add to this, that while divisions exist, there will always be found interested men who will not fail to support them; nor can we at all suppose that Satan will be idle to improve an advantage so important to the interests of his kingdom. And, let it be further observed upon the whole, that, in matters of similar importance to our secular interests, we would by no means content ourselves with such kind of reasoning. We might further add, that the attempt here suggested, not being of a partial, but of general nature, it can have no just tendency to excite the jealousy, or hurt the feelings of any part. On the contrary, every effort toward a permanent Scriptural unity among the churches, upon the solid basis of universally acknowledged and self-evident truths, must have the happiest tendency to enlighten and conciliate, by thus manifesting to each other their mutual charity and zeal for the truth: "Whom I love in the truth," saith the apostle, "and not I only, but also all they that have known the truth; for the truth's sake, which is in us, and shall be with us forever." Indeed, if no such Divine and adequate basis of union can be fairly exhibited, as will meet the approbation of every upright and intelligent Christian, nor such mode of procedure adopted in favour of the weak as will not oppress their consciences, then the accomplishment of this grand object upon principle must be forever impossible. There would, upon this supposition, remain no other way of accomplishing it, but merely by voluntary compromise, and good-natured accommodation. That such a thing, however, will be accomplished, one way or the other, will not be questioned by any that allow themselves to believe that the commands and prayers of our Lord Jesus Christ will not utterly prove ineffectual. Whatever way, then, it is to be effected, whether upon the solid basis of Divinely revealed truth, or the good-natured principle of Christian forbearance and gracious condescension, is it not equally practicable, equally eligible to us, as ever it can be to any; unless we should suppose ourselves destitute of that Christian temper and discernment which is essentially necessary to qualify us to do the will of our gracious Redeemer, whose express command to his people is, that there be "no divisions among them; but that they all walk by the same rule, speak the same thing, and be perfectly joined together in the same mind, and in the same judgment." We believe then it is as practicable as it is eligible. Let us attempt it. "Up, and be doing, and the Lord will be with us."

. . . For certainly the collective graces that are conferred upon the Church, if duly united and brought to bear upon any point of commanded duty, would be amply sufficient for the right and successful performance of it. "For to one is given by the Spirit the word of wisdom; to another the word of knowledge by the same Spirit; to another faith by the same Spirit; to another the discerning of spirits; but the manifestation of the Spirit is given to every man to profit withal. As every man, therefore, hath received the gift, even so minister the same one to another as good stewards of the manifold grace of God." In the face, then, of such instructions, and with such assurances of an all-sufficiency of Divine grace, as the Church has received from her exalted Head, we can neither justly doubt the concurrence of her genuine members; nor yet their ability, when dutifully acting together, to accomplish anything that is necessary for his glory, and their own good; and certainly their visible unity in truth and holiness, in faith and love, is, of all things, the most conducive to both these, if we may credit the dying commands and prayers of our gracious Lord. In a matter, therefore, of such confessed importance, our Christian brethren, however unhappily distinguished by party names, will not, cannot, withhold their helping hand. We are as heartily willing to be their debtors, as they are indispensably bound to be our benefactors. Come, then, dear brethren, we most humbly beseech you, cause your light to shine upon our weak beginnings, that we may see to work by it. Evince your zeal for the glory of Christ, and the spiritual welfare of your fellow Christians, by your hearty and zealous co-operation to promote the unity, purity, and prosperity of his Church.

Let none imagine that the subjoined propositions are at all intended as an overture toward a new creed or standard for the Church, or as in any wise designed to be made a term of communion; nothing can be further from our intention. They are merely designed for opening up the way, that we may come fairly and firmly to original ground upon clear and certain premises, and take up things just as the apostles left them; that thus disentangled from the accruing embarrassments of the intervening ages, we may stand with evidence upon the same ground on which the Church stood at the beginning. Having said so much to solicit attention and prevent mistake, we submit as follows:

1. That the Church of Christ upon earth is essentially, intentionally, and constitutionally one; consisting of all those in every place that profess their faith in Christ and obedience to him in all things according to the Scriptures, and that manifest the same by their tempers and conduct, and of none else; as none else can be truly and properly called Christians.

2. That although the Church of Christ upon earth must necessarily exist in particular and distinct societies, locally separate one from another, yet there ought to be no schisms, no uncharitable divisions among them. They ought to receive each other as Christ Jesus hath also received them, to the glory of God. And for this purpose they ought all to walk by the same rule, to mind and speak the same thing; and to be perfectly joined together in the same mind, and in the same judgment.

3. That in order to do this, nothing ought to be inculcated upon Christians as articles of faith; nor required of them as terms of communion, but what is expressly taught and enjoined upon them in the word of God. Nor ought anything to be admitted as of Divine obligation, in their Church constitution and managements, but what is expressly enjoined by the authority of our Lord Jesus Christ and his apostles upon the New Testament Church; either in express terms or by approved precedent.

4. That although the Scriptures of the Old and New Testaments are inseparably connected, making together but one perfect and entire revelation of the Divine will, for the edification and salvation of the Church, and therefor in that respect cannot be separated; yet as to what directly and properly belongs to their immediate object, the New Testament is as perfect a constitution for the worship, discipline, and government of the New Testament Church, and as perfect a rule for the particular duties of its members, as the Old Testament was for the worship, discipline, and government of the Old Testament Church, and the particular duties of its members.

5. That with respect to the commands and ordinances of our Lord Jesus Christ, where the Scriptures are silent as to the express time and manner of performance, if any such there be, no human authority has power to interfere, in order to supply the supposed deficiency by making laws for the Church; nor can anything more be required of Christians in such cases, but only that they so observe these commands and ordinances as will evidently answer the declared and obvious end of their institution. Much less has any human authority power to impose new commands or ordinances upon the Church, which our Lord Jesus Christ has not enjoined. Nothing ought to be received into the faith or worship of the Church, or to be made a term of communion among Christians, that is not as old as the New Testament.

6. That although inferences and deductions from Scripture premises, when fairly inferred, may be truly called the doctrine of God's holy word, yet are they not formally binding upon the consciences of Christians farther than they perceive the connection, and evidently see that they are so; for their faith must not stand in the wisdom of men, but in the power and veracity of God. Therefore, no such deductions can be made terms of communion, but do properly belong to the after and progressive edification of the Church. Hence, it is evident that no such deductions

or inferential truths ought to have any place in the Church's confession.

7. That although doctrinal exhibitions of the great system of Divine truths, and defensive testimonies in opposition to prevailing errors, be highly expedient, and the more full and explicit they be for these purposes, the better; yet, as these must be in a great measure the effect of human reasoning, and of course must contain many inferential truths, they ought not to be made terms of Christian communion; unless we suppose, what is contrary to fact, that none have a right to the communion of the Church, but such as possess a very clear and decisive judgment, or are come to a very high degree of doctrinal information; whereas the Church from the beginning did, and ever will, consist of little children and young men, as well as fathers.

8. That as it is not necessary that persons should have a particular knowledge or distinct apprehension of all Divinely revealed truths in order to entitle them a place in the Church; neither should they, for this purpose, be required to make a profession more extensive than their knowledge; but that, on the contrary, their having a due measure of Scriptural self-knowledge respecting their lost and perishing condition by nature and practice, and of the way of salvation through Jesus Christ, accompanied with a profession of their faith in and obedience to him, in all things, according to his word, is all that is absolutely necessary to qualify them for admission into his Church.

9. That all that are enabled through grace to make such a profession, and to manifest the reality of it in their tempers and conduct, should consider each other as the precious saints of God, should love each other as brethren, children of the same family and Father, temples of the same Spirit, members of the same body, subjects of the same grace, objects of the same Divine love, bought with the same price, and joint-heirs of the same inheritance. Whom God hath thus joined together no man should dare to put asunder.

10. That division among Christians is a horrid evil, fraught with many evils. It is antichristian, as it destroys the visible unity of the body of Christ; as if he were divided against himself, excluding and excommunicating a part of himself. It is antiscriptural, as being strictly prohibited by his sovereign authority; a direct violation of his express command. It is anti-natural, as it excites Christians to condemn, to hate, and oppose one another, who are bound by the highest and most endearing obligations to love each other as brethren, even as Christ has loved them. In a word, it is productive of confusion and of every evil work.

11. That (in some instances) a partial neglect of the expressly revealed will of God, and (in others) an assumed authority for making the approbation of human opinions and human inventions a term of communion, by introducing them into the constitution, faith, or worship of the Church, are, and have been, the immediate, obvious, and universally acknowledged causes of all the corruptions and divisions that ever have taken place in the Church of God.

12. That all that is necessary to the highest state of perfection and purity of the Church upon earth is, first, that none be received as members but such as having that due measure of Scriptural self-knowledge described above, do profess their faith in Christ and obedience to Him in all things according to the Scriptures; nor, secondly, that any be retained in her communion longer than they continue to manifest the reality of their profession by their tempers and conduct. Thirdly, that her ministers, duly and Scripturally qualified, inculcate none other things than those very articles of faith and holiness expressly revealed and enjoined in the word of God. Lastly, that in all their administrations they keep close by the observance of all Divine ordinances, after the example of the primitive Church, exhibited in the New Testament; without any additions whatsoever of human opinions or inventions of men.

13. Lastly. That if any circumstantials indispensably necessary to the observance of Divine ordinances be not found upon the page of express revelation, such, and such only, as are absolutely necessary for this purpose should be adopted under the title of human expedients, without any pretense to a more sacred origin, so that any subsequent alteration or difference in the observance of these things might produce no contention nor division in the Church.

From the nature and construction of these propositions, it will evidently appear, they are laid in a designed subserviency to the declared end of our association; and are exhibited for the express purpose of performing a duty of previous necessity, a duty loudly called for in existing circumstances at the hand of every one that would desire to promote the interests of Zion; a duty not only enjoined, as has been already observed from Isaiah lvii:14, but which is also there predicted of the faithful remnant as a thing in which they would voluntarily engage. "He that putteth his trust in me shall possess the land, and shall inherit my holy mountain; and shall say, Cast ye up, cast ye up, prepare the way; take up the stumbling block out of the way of my people."

To prepare the way for a permanent Scriptural unity among Christians, by calling up to their consideration fundamental truths, directing their attention to first principles, clearing the way before them by removing the stumbling blocks—the rubbish of ages, which has been thrown upon it, and fencing it on each side, that in advancing toward the desired object they may not miss the way through mistake or inadvertency, by turning aside to the right hand or to the left, is, at least, the sincere intention of the above propositions. It remains with our brethren now to say, how far they go toward answering this intention. Do they exhibit truths demonstrably evident in the light of Scripture and right reason, so that to deny any part of them the contrary assertion would be manifestly absurd and inadmissible? Considered as a preliminary for the above purpose, are they adequate, so that if acted upon, they would infallibly lead to the desired issue? If evidently defective in either of these respects, let them be corrected and amended, till they become sufficiently evident, adequate, and unexceptionable. In the meantime let them be examined with rigor, with all the rigor that justice, candor, and charity will admit. If we have mistaken the way, we shall be glad to be set right; but if, in the meantime we have been happily led to suggest obvious and undeniable truths, which, if adopted and acted upon, would infallibly lead to the desired unity, and secure it when obtained, we hope it will be no objection that they have not proceeded from a General Council. It is not the voice of the multitude, but the voice of truth, that has power with the conscience; that can produce rational conviction and acceptable obedience. A conscience that awaits the decision of the multitude, that hangs in suspense for the casting vote of the majority, is a fit subject for the man of sin. This, we are persuaded, is the uniform sentiment of real Christians of every denomination. Would to God that all professors were such, then should our eyes soon behold the prosperity of Zion; we should soon see Jerusalem a quiet habitation. Union in truth has been, and ever must be the desire and prayer of all such; "Union in Truth" is our motto.

Appendix B

EXCERPTS FROM
THE CHRISTIAN SYSTEM[1]
by
Alexander Campbell, 1837

"I pray. . .for those who shall believe on me through their teaching, *that all may be one*; that as thou, Father, art in me, and I in thee, *they also may be in us, that the world may believe* that thou hast sent me, and that thou gavest me the glory, which I have given them, that *they may be one*, as we are one; I in them, and thou in me, *that their union may be perfected*: and that *the world may know* that thou hast sent me, and that thou lovest them as thou lovest me." Thus Messiah prayed; and well might he pray thus, seeing he was wise enough to teach that, If a kingdom be torn by factions, that kingdom can not subsist. And if a family be torn by factions, that family can not subsist. By civil dissensions any kingdom may be desolated; and no city or family, where such dissensions are, can subsist."

If this be true—and true it is, if Jesus be the Messiah, in what moral desolation is the kingdom of Jesus Christ! Was there at any time, or is there now, in all the earth, a

---

[1]Alexander Campbell, *The Christian System* (reprinted, Nashville: Gospel Advocate Company, 1980), pp. 84-87. Originally published in 1837.

kingdom more convulsed by internal broils and dissensions, than what is commonly called the church of Jesus Christ? Should any one think it lawful to paganize both the Greek and Latin churches—to eject one hundred millions of members of the Greek and Roman communions from the visible and invisible precincts of the Christian family or kingdom of Jesus Christ, and regard the Protestant faith and people as the only true faith and the only true citizens of the kingdom of Jesus; what then shall we say of them, contemplated as the visible kingdom over which Jesus presides as Prophet, Priest, and King? Of forty millions of Protestants shall we constitute the visible kingdom of the Prince of Peace? Be it so for the sake of argument; and what then? The Christian army is forty millions strong; but how do they muster? Under forty ensigns? Under forty antagonistic leaders? Would to God there were but forty! In the Geneva detachment alone there is almost that number of petty chiefs. My soul sickens at the details!

Take the English branch of the Protestant faith—I mean England and the United States and all the islands where the English Bible is read; and how many broils, dissensions, and anathemas may we compute? I will not attempt to name the antagonizing creeds, feuds, and parties that are in eternal war, under the banners of the Prince of Peace. And yet they talk of love and charity, and of the conversion of the Jews, the Turks, and Pagans!!!

Shall we turn from the picture, lay down our pen, and languish in despair? No: for Jesus has said, "Happy the *peacemakers*, for they shall be called *sons of God*." But who can make peace when all the elements are at war? Who so enthusiastic as to fancy that he can stem the torrent of strife or quench the violence of sectarian fire? But the page of universal history whispers in our ears, "If you tarry till all the belligerent armies lay down their arms and make one spontaneous and simultaneous effort to unite, you will be as very a simpleton as he that sat by the Euphrates waiting till all its waters ran into the sea."

. . . From Messiah's intercession above quoted, it is incontrovertible that union is strength, and disunion weakness; that there is a plan founded in infinite wisdom and love, by which, and by which alone, the world may both *believe* and *know* that God has sent his Son to be the Saviour of the world; and, like all the schemes of Heaven, it is simple to admiration. No mortal need fancy that he shall have the honor of devising either the plan of uniting Christians in one holy band of zealous co-operation, or of converting Jews and Gentiles to the faith that Jesus is that <u>seed</u> in whom all the families of the earth are yet to be blessed. The plan is divine. Is any one impatient to hear it? Let him again read the intercessions of the Lord Messiah, which we have chosen for our motto. Let him then examine the two following propositions, and say whether these do not express Heaven's own scheme of augmenting and conservating the body of Christ.

First: *Nothing is essential to the conversion of the world but the union and cooperation of Christians.*
Second: *Nothing is essential to the union of Christians but the apostles' teaching or testimony.*

Or does he choose to express the plan of the Self-Existent in other words? Then he may change the order, and say—

First: *The testimony of the apostles is the only and all-sufficient means of uniting all Christians.*
Second: *The union of Christians with the apostles' testimony is all-sufficient and alone sufficient to the conversion of the world.*

Neither truth alone nor union alone is sufficient to subdue the unbelieving nations; but truth and union combined are omnipotent. They are omnipotent, for God is in them and with them, and has consecrated and blessed them for this very purpose.

These two propositions have been stated, illustrated, developed (and shall I say proved?) in the *Christian Baptist*, and *Millennial Harbinger*, to the conviction of thousands. Indeed one of them is as universally conceded as it has been proposed, viz.: *That the union of Christians is essential to the conversion of the world*; and though, perhaps some might be found who would question whether, if all Christians were united, the whole world could be converted to God; there is no person, of whom we have heard, who admits a general of universal prevalence of the gospel, in what is usually called the millennial age of the world, and who admits that moral means will have anything to do with its introduction, who does not also admit that the union of Christians is essential to that state of things. Indeed, to suppose that all Christians will form one communion in that happy age of the world, and not before it, is to suppose a moral effect without a cause.

The second proposition, viz.: *That the word or testimony of the apostles is itself all-sufficient and alone sufficient to the union of all Christians,* can not be rationally doubted by any person acquainted with that testimony, or who admits the competency of their inspiration to make them infallible teachers of the Christian institution. And, indeed, all who contend for those human institutions called creeds contend for them as necessary only to the existence of a party, or while the present schisms, contentions, and dissensions exist. Therefore, all the defenses of creeds, ancient and modern, while they assert the Bible alone is the only perfect and infallible rule of faith and morals, not only concede that these symbols called creeds are imperfect and fallible, but also that these *creeds* never can achieve what the Bible, without them, can accomplish.

152

Appendix C

EXCERPTS FROM
THE QUEST FOR HOLINESS AND UNITY[1]
by
John W. V. Smith, 1980

One item with major unresolved issues for the future of
the Church of God movement comes under the general
heading of relationships. In light of the movement's central emphasis on Christian unity, these issues become particularly important. It must be remembered that, despite
its strong irenic focus, the Church of God was born and
developed in a very polemic atmosphere. Enemies were
readily and specifically identified—even invited. Attacks
by and on these adversaries were vigorous and frequent.
If, as many sociologists affirm, a certain degree of conflict
is essential to group formation and growth, then the early
Church of God movement had the basic ingredients for a
solid self-identity and rapid expansion. Unity as a doctrine or an ideal for the church was itself a source of conflict because it was opposed by loyal "sectarians" who were
offended by the call to "come-out" of their denominations
and stand together in an open fellowship of the Spirit. In

---

[1]John W.V. Smith, *The Quest for Holiness and Unity* (Anderson, IN:
Warner Press, 1980), pp. 439-443. This is the narrative history of the
Church of God movement (Anderson) published on the occasion of the
movement's centennial celebration.

this context the message of Christian unity was a call to action and combat.

Then the religious climate began to change after 1910 when the glow of ecumenism sparked by the Edinburgh Missionary Conference began to grow brighter and burst into a light by 1948 with the formation of the World Council of Churches—a development in which the Church of God had been totally uninvolved. For this movement it might have been thought of as having won a war without having been in a single battle, but that was not the case. The launching of a worldwide ecumenical movement was not regarded as a victory, and there was not rejoicing over the fact that a great segment of Christendom had come to the point of openly questing for the same goal the Church of God had upheld for two-thirds of a century. Instead, the changing external climate sparked the beginning of a time of internal assessment within the movement itself.

The Church of God movement had lost its enemies and with their passing came a sense of wonderment resulting from the erosion of a sharp definition of identity and purpose. This condition set off an avalanche of self-analysis studies by young Church of God scholars. The popular response to what was happening outside the Church of God was for it [the Church of God movement] to become critical of the ecumenical movement regarding its methodology, for its truncated view of union rather than unity, and, along with other conservative evangelicals, for its involvement in social and political issues. In the ultimate sense, however, there could be no denying that the Church of God and the cooperating "sinful sectarians" were aiming at the same target.

To complicate the situation, the noncooperative stance of the Church of God led it to a position of relative aloneness in the Christian world. At the same time that the movement was losing its enemies, it was not cultivating many close friends. . . . There were no real allies to join forces with in doing battle with the major evils of the world. So at its first century's end [1980] the movement found itself with a rather fuzzy identity as related to the rest of Christianity, without specifically identified enemies and without any formally declared friends. In this uncomfortable context it is difficult to find exciting ways to give emphasis to the doctrine of Christian unity.

In facing this situation the Church of God movement has several options. At least four possible courses regarding its unity stance seem to be open to the movement as it looks toward the future.

Option One. The first option is simply to continue as in the past—preach unity vigorously, get emotional about the biblical vision of the one holy church, write articles and books about it, tell others that "we believe in it," and then wait for it to happen, taking little or no responsibility to implement it or further its achievement. Stated this way, such a position appears idealistic, even dreamy and unrealistic. This, many would quickly say, is the best way to insure that Christian unity will never be realized. The voice of practicality would say that such a stance should be altered and that the movement should quickly find ways to become involved in the multitude of opportunities to further the cause of unity.

On the other hand, there still is the possibility that there may be some validity to what Church of God leaders have been saying for many years about being "leaven in the lump," about being dedicated to a "unity of the Spirit" approach, and about the inadequacies inherent in the federation or council-of-churches path to unity. It could be that the nonjoining stance might be, in the long run, a greater witness to real unity than to be linked on a marginal basis with many other groups. Careful scrutiny and evaluation might determine that the historic stance is an option that is both tenable and defensible or that only slight modifications need to be made.

Option Two. The second option would be to seek out compatible allies and work with them in all ways that would enhance the spread of the gospel and increase the impact of the church's mission in the world.[2] This is already being done in selected areas such as curriculum, foreign missions, and stewardship education. The possibilities for enlarging these cooperative arrangements are almost infinite. Such a posture allows a high degree of selectivity regarding both what and with whom such relationships are established. Probably it would cut costs and increase overall effectiveness in the cooperative areas. If this option were selected, the movement's aloneness would be mitigated. It would be possible to do this without violating the nonjoining principle. It is a viable option, but obviously not a major step on the road to Christian unity. Such arrangements are nice, but they really do little to solve the deep problem of Christian disunity.

Option Three. Another option would be to reassess the historic nonjoining stance and to affiliate with selected interdenominational organizations with which the movement could feel comfortable. The long and often advanced argument that the Church of God cannot join any organization because its polity does not provide for any corporate body which has authority over the various congregations would need to be dealt with in such a manner that it would be clear to all just what commitments were being made. The General Assembly itself could join any of these ecumenical organizations, and it is true that this would not obligate any congregation to any greater extent than it desired—a condition which is true for any action of the Assembly. This would pose no problem for any of the ecumenical organizations, for they would simply list the General Assembly of the Church of God as a member rather than the Church of God. Properly understood, it should pose no problem for the movement either.

Once this hurdle was passed, the next big question

---

[2]This option is the one now being taken as the Church of God and the Christian Churches/Churches of Christ are intentional about building mutual awareness and appreciation and discovering ways that church mission can be engaged in more effectively if done together.

would be which interdenominational group(s) to join. Unfortunately, there are competitive and rival councils and associations. Theologically, the Church of God movement would find greater affinity with groups such as the National Association of Evangelicals and the Christian Holiness Association, and there has been considerable involvement of Church of God persons in the meetings and continuing programs of groups like these. On the other hand, there has been an even longer involvement in program departments, divisions, commissions, and committees of the National Council of Churches. Recent restructuring within this body has eroded the opportunities for nonmembers to be included, so that participation there has been considerably lessened in recent years. Even so, relationships have been good and the spirit of openness and freedom of expression have created good feelings on the part of participants even though there might be strong disagreement with some National Council pronouncements and programs. . . .

Option Four. There is one other possible option. Being a Christian unity movement, the Church of God could enter the ecumenical arena "full blast"—joining *all* interdenominational organizations whose "basis" would not require a compromise of cardinal biblical teachings. Standing where it does in the theological spectrum, and with relatively wide acquaintance already in the various camps, the Church of God may be in the unique position of serving as a bridge across the wide chasms created by these polarized clusters in national and world Christianity. The full implications of such a move are difficult even to imagine, but it is an option and all the avenues of reformation have not yet been traveled. It would take a great deal of finesse—and courage—to make this choice and act upon it.

Appendix D

PRESENTATION TO THE "OPEN FORUM"[1]

by Michael Kinnamon
March 16, 1988

Dear sisters and brothers in Christ. It is a privilege and pleasure to speak to you this evening, to share in your discussions about the future of the church. That does not mean, however, that everything I say will please you. The very theme of this evening's forum disturbs me a bit for reasons that I think will become clear. But I share my thoughts—even the disturbing ones—not as a stranger but as a brother in the faith. I will never learn all of your names, but I am absolutely convinced that all of us here (indeed, all who confess Christ around the world) are related to each other by blood—the blood of Christ which was shed equally for us all and which flows through our common body each time we gather around our family table.

---

[1]As a prominent leader among the Disciples of Christ and an experienced participant in the ecumenical movement, Michael Kinnamon was invited to address a group of leaders from the Christian Churches/ Churches of Christ on the topic of Christian unity. This is the presentation he delivered. Used by permission. Among his significant publications is *Truth and Community: Diversity and Its Limits in the Ecumenical Movement.*

In the time given me, I want to make three main points. They are as follows, with each considered only briefly.

1. If we are serious about spreading our pleas for unity, then it is essential that we overcome the present disunity of the Restorationist Movement. It is an old story: the credibility of our message is weakened by the non-credibility of the messengers. Having set out to serve as a catalyst for unity among Christians, the Campbell-Stone movement has managed to contribute at least three new churches to the bewildering and disheartening array of denominations in American Christianity. We—Disciples, Independents, and Churches of Christ—have institutionalized our disobedience to Christ's prayer that all his followers may be one. We, thereby, have betrayed our calling to participate in God's plan to reconcile all things in heaven and on earth.

Let me put it another way. One of the insights of our common ancestors—the Campbells and Barton Stone— was that the church proclaims the truth of God, and thus challenges the false gods of this world, not just by what it *says* or *does*, but by what it *is*. The apostle Paul certainly knew this too. Throughout his letters he insists that the very existence of the church—in which Jews and Gentiles walk together—can be a sign to the world (with its powers and principalities) of God's reconciling purpose and power. The witness of the New Testament Church did not stem so much from what it *did* (as a small, politically-powerless band), but from what it *was*—a body which through God's Spirit united former enemies, Jews and Greeks, people of fundamental differences, around the living truth of Jesus Christ.

In the same way, our movement was to be a sign to the rest of Christianity of the church's calling to be one people. But what kind of sign have we become? If anything, our fragmented movement says to the world that Jesus Christ is not a sufficient center to hold us together in the face of human disagreements—and that, friends, makes what we have become blasphemous! Tonight's theme speaks of

160

"strategies," (i.e., things we can do), but surely the best way to further our pleas for unity is to *be* what we wish *to proclaim.*

Of course, all of this is easier said than done! But the way to begin, I'm convinced, is with mutual confession of the way we have offended each other (especially by caricaturing) and with an admission that we need each other. In saying that, I am reminded of a line by the Roman Catholic theologian, Hans Küng. The person, says Küng, who preaches half the gospel is no less a heretic than the person who preaches the other half. There is no doubt that Disciples have preached and lived less than the full gospel. For example, we have, in my opinion, paid too little attention to the invitational dimension of evangelism, to the spiritual alienation of persons from God. We have also failed to make clear to ourselves or others the central place of Scripture in our reflections on the faith. I leave it to you to make your own confessions. But, in general, I think we can say that the ecumenically-involved churches (like the Disciples) tend to dismiss more evangelical churches as being interested only in their own vision of truth at the expense of unity, while the more evangelical churches (like the Independent Christians) tend to dismiss the ecumenical churches as being interested only in their vision of unity at the expense of truth. Surely the one church of Jesus Christ is to be both evangelical and ecumenical—both aggressive in its proclamation and humble in its love. We need each other!

2. Now I will be more controversial, though I hope you will remember the spirit in which I speak. The next suggestion I have for "penetrating Christianity" with the vision of unity is simple, to participate in the hard work of dialogue with other churches, dialogue generally carried on through what is called the ecumenical movement. Let me read to you three brief statements.

The restoration of unity among all Christians is one of the principle concerns of this council. Christ the Lord

161

founded one Church and one Church only. . . . Our present division openly contradicts the will of Christ, scandalizes the world, and damages that most holy cause, the preaching of the gospel to every creature.

We affirm our devotion to one God, the Father of our Lord Jesus Christ, and our membership in the holy, catholic church, which is greater than any single church and than all churches together. We believe that denominations exist not for themselves, but as parts of that Church, within which each denomination is to live and labor, and, if need be, die.

The purpose of our union is the carrying out of God's will as this is expressed in our Lord's prayer "That they may all be one that the world may believe that Thou didst send me." [Our hope is that we may be] a true leaven of unity in the life of this country. . .and we seek the unity of the spirit in the bond of peace with all Christians.

The first statement comes from the *Decree on Ecumenism* written by the Roman Catholic Church at its Second Vatican Council in 1964; the second comes from the *Basis of Union* of the United Church of Christ; and the third comes from the *Constitution* of the Church of South India. I could multiply such statements almost endlessly because it is hard to find a single ecumenically-involved church that does not profess a central, biblically-grounded concern for unity (indeed, they take it as part of their mission to promote unity among Christians), and many of them are acting on that conviction through participation in councils of churches, theological dialogues, and cooperative programs. And I have to ask: Why aren't you [Independent Christians] more involved?

I must admit that my first response to tonight's theme was to be utterly overwhelmed by the audacity of it. You ask, "How can *we* penetrate other churches with *our* pleas for unity," while around the world churches representing well over one billion Christians are every day engaged in activities aimed at growing in deeper fellowship together! I can't tell you how many conversations I have had through the World Council of Churches with representatives of other churches who wanted to know from me how Independent Christians could be encouraged to join in the search for unity. You see, for most of the Christian world, you [Independent Christians] are seen as the ones who need to hear the plea—because, while you talk about a passion for unity (which other churches share), you remain too often on the sidelines.

I am reminded of a story about the Danish philosopher Søren Kierkegaard. According to the story, Kierkegaard was walking down a street in Copenhagen when he saw a sign that said "Pants pressed here." Kierkegaard went in and began to take off his pants, until the shopkeeper came rushing out to say, "I don't press pants; I just paint signs!" Right now, the Independent Christian Churches seem basically to be sign painters, or so it looks to many other Christians. Growing in unity, building trust among those whom Christ has embraced, is never easy or "clean." It doesn't just happen on our terms. Like pressing pants, it is hard work; but all of the churches have got to get in and do it.

At this point I need to make an important admission: the various instruments of the ecumenical movement, e.g., the World Council of Churches, may not always be faithful or effective instruments for achieving Christian oneness. The WCC, to continue this one example, has done some remarkable work in bringing Christians together. I have no doubt at all that through these efforts we have often seen the working of the Holy Spirit. But at other times the Council (in my opinion) seems in danger of succumbing to a kind of works' righteousness which identifies the boundaries of Christian communion with certain social-political commitments. Some of its statements sound as if ecumenism were a new orthodoxy of the left-wing instead of a commitment to search for truth in diverse community. So, if you have questions about the Council, so do I.

Worse yet, Disciples have at times seemed to equate being ecumenical with support for all things done by the

WCC! The WCC, the National Council of Churches, the Consultation on Church Union, and other ecumenical instruments, like all human organizations, must continually be challenged and measured by the vision of the gospel. But, in order to do such challenging and measuring, you have got to be involved—and not just for your sake, but also for mine and other Christians. The Disciples and other branches of the Christian tree need the witness of the Independent Christians.

3. Ecumenical growth takes place, the plea is heard, only when there is genuine humility of the Spirit. The ecumenical vision, as I understand it, rests ultimately on the sovereignty of God. All human claims to truth stand under judgment of the One who alone is holy, the One who transcends all of our projects and explanations. "For my thoughts are not your thoughts, neither are your ways my ways, says the Lord."

One of the best expressions of this is surely the first two commandments from Sinai. The first commandment (no other gods) tells us that our faith must be in the Truth above all truths, the one Jesus called Father. But the second commandment (no graven images) immediately reminds us that our perceptions of that truth are never final. The Bible worries about golden calves; today we need to beware of graven-image theologies which idolatrously claim to present full verbal pictures of God. The point is that we are God's, not that God is ours. Our task is to conform to God's will, not to insist that everyone else conform to ours—our way of baptizing, our view of mission, our form of church government, our decision about who is saved.

Let me put this in terms of our heritage. It is one thing to argue, as Thomas Campbell did, for a return to the simplicity of New Testament faith and to require no more; it is quite another to claim to have restored the "ancient order of things" and to allow no less—which is why the plea has often not been heard. If the plea is for Christians to search together for the fullness of the gospel around which we can and must unify, that is one thing. If the plea is for "them" to recognize that "we" already possess the truth of the gospel in its fullness and that unity means joining with us on our terms, then that is quite another. The weakness in Thomas Campbell's plea for unity, as I see it, was the unwarranted assumption that most Christians could easily agree on what is essential. The flaw in the thinking of many who followed him was an unwillingness to recognize their own conclusions as "opinion," to acknowledge that different conclusions about the gospel can be drawn by others of good faith who look to the Bible for guidance.

Yes, Scripture is our touchstone, our authority. But even if we regard it as inerrant, even if we overlook the great diversity Scripture encompasses, we need to recognize that people read Scripture through glasses that are shaped by their cultures, their churches, their moments in history. That is why one of the more important things about Scripture is the people with whom we read it. We are the undeserving recipients of God's grace, not the definitive possessors of it, and, thus, if we are serious about being the church God wills, we need each other precisely because we see from different angles. Jesus did not leave us a text; he left us a community which comes to know God's will and shows forth God's purposes not by the purity of its thoughts and practices, but by the visible reality of its love. That is why I think the Roman Catholic Church's Vatican II (1962-1965) was exactly right when it wrote these words:

> There can be no ecumenism of the name without a change of heart. For it is from newness of attitudes, from self-denial and unstinted love, that yearnings for unity take their rise and grow towards maturity. We should pray to the Spirit for the grace to be genuinely self-denying, humble, gentle in the service of others, and to have an attitude of brotherly generosity toward them.

It is no secret that the world is filled with what can only be called mean-spiritedness. It is apparently part of

the human character to justify "the way we are" by surrounding ourselves with those who are "like us." As a
result, society is filled with like-minded clubs and same-
colored neighborhoods. But the Scriptural mandate of the
church is to be something else. Paul's letter to the Romans
represents a mighty attempt to show that God is not
served by the victory of Jewish-Christians over Gentile-
Christians, or vice versa, but by their willingness to live
trustfully with differences, as a result of their common
faith in Christ. Therefore, Paul exclaims, "welcome one
another as Christ has welcomed you, to the glory of God."
If we were able to welcome one another—Protestant and
Catholic, liberal and conservative, black and white,
Russian and American, Disciples and Independents—then
we would give glory to God. And that would be the most
eloquent statement possible of our historic plea for
Christian unity.

Appendix E

EXCERPT FROM CELEBRATION OF HERITAGE[1]

by
Robert Oldham Fife, 1992

Paul exhorted the Ephesians to "make every effort to keep the unity of the Spirit in the bond of peace" (Eph. 4:1). He is not here referring to the unity of a good attitude, important though that may be. Rather, he is speaking of that unity which is the creation of the Holy Spirit through the Gospel of Christ's reconciling work on the Cross (Eph. 3:14-18). That Spirit-created unity may always be discerned by the seven marks which Paul lists—One Body, One Spirit, One Hope, One Lord, One Faith, One Baptism, One God and Father.

Like the Ephesians, we are to "*keep* the unity of the Spirit." This is both a reminder and a command. The reminder is that the unity of the Spirit cannot be contrived or arranged. Rather, it is the *Gift* of God. It came upon the Jerusalem Church as God's doing, for "the *Lord* added to their number daily those who were being saved"

---

[1]Robert Oldham Fife, *Celebration of Heritage* (privately printed, 1992), pp. 190-194. From "The Nature of Christian Unity," a paper presented at "Restoration Forum V," Cincinnati, Ohio, on April 30, 1987. The "Restoration Forums" are a series of annual discussions held since 1983 between the Christian Churches/Churches of Christ and the Churches of Christ (non-instrumental).

(Acts 2:41, 47). The Ephesian Jews and Gentiles were reminded that it was Jesus who had reconciled "them both in one body unto God through the Cross" (Eph. 2:16). Christian unity is the necessary consequence of one simple fact: In reconciling us to Himself, God joins us to one another.

All of us are included in the unity which the Holy Spirit created on Pentecost, and continues to create through the terms of the Covenant there enunciated by the apostles. In response to that Good News we were immersed into the body of Christ (1 Cor. 12:13) and discovered each other. We did not primarily join each other. We joined Jesus. But in His gracious wisdom, the Lord was not content to extend His fellowship unto us in isolation from each other. Therefore, He "added" us to one another. Because this was His doing, we have no power to "unjoin" one another, save as one may be severed from Jesus. We have received the Gift of unity through our appropriation of the redeeming and reconciling sacrifice of our dear Lord. That Gift we are charged to keep—yes, to treasure. "What God has joined together, let man not separate!" (Mt. 19:6).

But what of those differences which have historically sundered our fellowship, and even now deprive us of the blessings of mutual encouragement? These differences cannot be treated as insignificant, for they involve convictions held in conscience. Indeed, many of us have chosen not to acknowledge the Gift of unity if it involves fellowship with those we deem to be "in error." But the trouble is that there is hardly a leader among us who is not considered by someone else to be "in error." So we have "pulled our cloaks around us," lest association with others be taken as endorsement of their error. Would we have condemned Jesus for eating with sinners? (Mk. 2:16; Lk. 7:34).

Is it not ironic that Christ would die for us "while we were sinners" (Rom. 5:8), but we will not live with each other while one is "in error?" If God's grace and forbearance towards us sinners did not compromise Him, are we compromised when we extend grace and forbearance to baptized believers whom we consider to be "in error?" Jesus had something to say about debtors who receive grace from their Master, but who demand the last farthing from others (Mt. 18:21).

What are we then to do? Shall we go with those who claim that their particular group is "the only true Church" —thus adding restrictive tests to the seven universal marks of the unity of the Spirit? Or, shall we join those discouraged ones who have abandoned the quest of unity as "dreaming the impossible dream"?

Neither of these alternatives is biblical. The glorious Church of our Lord Jesus Christ is far greater than any particular group among us. On the other hand, discouraged though some may be, we dare not abandon our responsibility for unity as though it were an "impossible dream." It is no "dream" that our Lord has already made us one in the blood of the Cross! (Eph. 2:13-18).

What shall we then do? We need to recover the Biblical truth that there are two dimensions to Christian unity. These are clearly set forth in the Ephesian letter. There we learn that Christian unity is not only a *Gift* to be treasured; it is also a *Goal* to be attained.

We have already noticed Paul's exhortation to the Ephesians to "keep the unity of the Spirit." He then declares that the ascended Lord gave gifts of ministry

> to prepare God's people for works of service, so that the body of Christ may be built up until we all reach unity in the faith and in the knowledge of the Son of God and become mature, attaining the whole measure of the fulness of Christ. (Eph. 4:12, 13)

"Unity in the *faith* and in the *knowledge* of the Son of God" has ever been the Goal of the Church. But neither in the days of the apostles nor in our own has this Goal of the "measure of the stature of the fulness of Christ" been attained. We are one in our faith—in our earnest personal and corporate commitment to the Lord Jesus Christ. But it is obvious that we are not yet one in the "knowledge" which grows out of our faith.

What then? Shall we reject the Gift of the unity of the Spirit until we shall have obtained the Goal of unity in a common faith-knowledge? Can it be before "we all" (which includes brothers yet unknown to us) "attain the measure of the stature of the fulness of Christ"? Must the blessings of fellowship await that glorious consummation?

The simple fact is that we are yet disciples—learners. Some of us may have greater comprehension than others, but not one of us "knows it all." Therefore, just as our Lord was Himself "full of grace and truth" (Jn. 1:14), we are exhorted to "grow in grace and in knowledge of our Lord and Saviour Jesus Christ" (2 Pet. 3:18). But how can any of us grow if we have nothing to do with each other? If I only have fellowship with those who think as I do, I not only deprive others of what I may have to teach; I also rob myself of what I might learn. Or if I think I have "nothing to learn," I probably have not learned one preeminent truth: Even those of us who are impeccably "right" are still saved by grace.

The Ephesian congregation was exhorted to "*keep* the unity of the Spirit in the bond of peace," while seeking to "*attain* the unity of the faith and of the knowledge of the Son of God." We are under the same mandate.

Appendix F

EXCERPT FROM CONTOURS OF A CAUSE: THE THEOLOGICAL VISION OF THE CHURCH OF GOD MOVEMENT (ANDERSON)[1]

by
Barry L. Callen, 1995

One important focus of the praying of Jesus was that his disciples of all times would experience and practice a unity among themselves like exists between God the Father and the Son Jesus (John 17). Such an experience and practice has been a central goal of the Church of God (Anderson) movement.

Many Christian traditions have identified classic "marks" of the church that God intends. These marks are holy, catholic, apostolic, and one. The Church of God movement has affirmed all of these, including the last as a natural outcome of the others. God founded only one church (Jn. 10:16; 21:15; Eph. 5:27) and believers are expected to make every effort to maintain its unity in the Spirit (Eph. 4:3-4). The New Testament does speak of churches (plural), meaning only that each is a local extension and expression of the one body united in Jesus Christ, its head, and empowered by the one indwelling Spirit, its life.

---

[1]Barry Callen, *Contours of a Cause: Theological Vision of the Church of God (Anderson)*, 158-168. Used by permission.

This church of God is understood biblically as both the universal church and any local assembly (congregation) of the whole. The church by definition is one (Eph. 2:11-21; 4:1-16). The oneness is to be expressed in each local assembly since each is intended to be a visible appearance of the whole in a given time and place. What an awesome and demanding thought! A congregation belonging to God is to represent the whole church in its particular geographic place. It is the church catholic that is to celebrate, model, and proclaim the good news in its community. All functions of the church and all dimensions of the good news belong in each place. When a congregation baptizes a new believer, for instance, that baptism should be into the *whole church*, not into a cut-off piece of it. The fellowship of the church should evidence an overcoming of human cultural, gender, and racial barriers. Paul says that Jesus brings *shalom* to human hatreds, peace "to you who were far away" (Gentiles) and "to those who were near" (Jews) (Eph. 2:17).

Unity is a crucial mark of the church. Division confuses, weakens, alienates, and thereby hampers mission. Where unity is understood as a dynasty of successor male bishops (apostolic succession), it is oppressive and strangles appropriate diversity and plurality. On the other hand, ecumenism, the quest for the realization of Christian unity, contrasts with the competitive mentality seen commonly in human societies. Accordingly:

> Ecumenism is a way of looking at reality that refuses to absolutize relative perspectives. It is an approach to knowledge which insists that truth is seldom discovered in isolation but rather through dialogue in diverse community. It is a way of living that dares to think globally and live trustfully with differences in community, not as a result of polite tolerance but on the basis of our common commitment to and experience of the creating, redeeming, and sustaining God.[2]

---

[2]Michael Kinnamon, *Truth and Community*, 109.

172

While Christian unity is a gift from God through the Spirit, it is realized only as Christians intentionally open themselves to be in community with other believers.[3] "Unity is given," according to James Earl Massey, "but our experience of it must be gained." The givenness roots in the fact that "the church is the community of those who honor Jesus Christ, sharing his life, teachings, and work. Belonging to him makes every believer belong to all other believers."[4] But what of the persistent dividedness among Christ's people? Believers typically experience the fellowship of God's people in connection with some denominational body. Is this fact division by definition? There appears to exist a perplexing paradox: the multiplicity of Christian traditions is due in part to human sin (Gal. 5:19-21) and in part to the inevitable varieties of human cultures, symbol systems, and historical circumstances that are not sinful in themselves.

We have to face the question: "How may a people who

---

[3]What constitutes true and viable Christian unity? Must there be full agreement on beliefs, or a single organizational network, or is the goal more in the area of attitudes? Early leaders of the Church of God movement (Anderson) envisioned denominational structures collapsing (not merging). For the most part that has not happened. Consideration now should be given to this judgment of Emil Brunner: "Certain as is the fact that a number of competing churches represents a scandal, equally certain is it on the other hand that a variety of forms of Christian fellowship is a necessity. . . . Far more important than organizational reunion of the historical churches is the readiness of individual Christians . . . to cooperate in a spirit of brotherliness" (*The Misunderstanding of the Church*, Philadelphia: Westminster Press, 1953, 112).

[4]James Earl Massey, *Concerning Christian Unity* (Anderson, IN: Warner Press, 1979), 8, 11, 20. Clark Williamson adds that "unity in the church, fragmentarily but really, is where the diverse members of the body of Christ are aware of and appreciate their essential relatedness to each other, where they love one another with the kind of love with which they have been loved" (*A Guest in the House of Israel*, Louisville: Westminster/John Knox Press, 1993, 262). James Evans, Jr., says that "the solidarity of that community (koinonia of the church). . .is strong enough to render all other stratifications among human beings of only secondary importance. Thus in the holy community 'there is no Greek nor Jew, slave nor free, male nor female'" (*We Have Been Believers: An African-American Systematic Theology*, Minneapolis: Augsburg Fortress, 1992, 136).

exist as a distinct community within the Church, for the sake of witness unto the unity of the Church, avoid the negation of their witness by their very existence?"[5] To avoid just such a negation, in 1804 there was published *The Last Will and Testament of the Springfield Presbytery* to explain why a reforming Christian group would dissolve its own interim "church" body, would "die the death" organizationally as a witness to Christian unity. "We will," it boldly announced, "that this body die, be dissolved, and sink into union with the Body of Christ at large; for there is but one Body and one Spirit, even as we are called in one hope of our calling."[6]

Can an identifiable Christian body successfully "sink" into the whole of God's people as a unity witness without disappearing and thus forfeiting any real base from which to witness to and help realize Christian unity? Is the divisiveness of our denominationalized Christian community so assumed and entrenched, so sociologically inevitable, that there is no alternative? Because of the hurtfulness of division to the church's mission and because the New Testament witness highlights the goal of Christian unity, even presents it as the personal prayer of Jesus on behalf of all his disciples in all times (John 17), many Christians over the centuries have affirmed that there must be an alternative to rampant division.[7] A movement that serves to upbuild the church, not divide and tear down, may be seen as a gift of the Spirit to the church.

For the Kentucky Christians led by Barton Stone and his colleagues, *The Last Will and Testament* declared an intentional "sinking" by no longer defining Christian fellowship in terms of a particular institution to which all

[5]Robert Oldham Fife, "The Neglected Alternative" in *Celebration of Heritage*, 265.

[6]This document, written by Barton W. Stone, is a classic in the "Restorationist" movement.

[7]Theodore Jennings insists that "division is a problem for the identity of the church. Division is a sign of the power of the world and sin. Division is then the antisign (the countersign) to the reign of God" (*Loyalty To God*, Nashville: Abingdon Press, 1992, 188).

Christians could not belong. These visionary reformers sought to become a microcosm of the whole church, with no other criteria of unity except those which can be the bond of unity for the whole church. There would be no restrictive creed mandated on all members. Evangelizing should be done *as the church* (the whole body of Christ) and for the church. Baptizing would be into the church, not into a given segment of it. The invitation to the Lord's Supper would be issued as representatives of the whole body to any in the body wishing to participate (it is, after all, the Lord's table, not ours).

How, then, should one describe groupings of Christians that seek to represent and serve the whole church in distinctive ways, without claiming for themselves those characteristics belonging only to the whole body? One helpful distinction is that between the church and "movements" within it. Affirming that the church is one and that such oneness is obscured when denominations divide the church into "churches," Robert Fife defines a "movement" as "a community of understanding and concern which exists and serves within the Church, and for its edification."[8]

Sometimes particular groupings of Christians come into being because their members share certain understandings and concerns about the faith.[9] Such distinctive communities *within* the church (not *as* the church) help facilitate the internal dialogue of the church as the whole body seeks its maturity and unity for the sake of its mission.[10] Movements,

---

[8]Robert Fife, *Celebration of Heritage*, 276.

[9]Even within the New Testament we already see early approaches to understanding a unity in plurality within the church (diversity of spiritual gifts, the Christian conscience and "gray areas," cultural diversity implied in the reality of multiple congregations, their differing settings and range of approaches to problems). In each case, unity left room for some diversity. See Rex Koivisto, *One Lord, One Faith*, 37-42.

[10]Robert Fife, *Celebration of Heritage*, 265-271. Fife calls for denominations to cease calling themselves "churches" and assuming for themselves the dignity and prerogatives belonging only to the church (274). In this regard, note C.C. Morrison, editor of the *Christian Century*, 77:10 (March 9, 1960), 281.

therefore, are "characteristic of the church as a living organism." They are actions of the body of Christ rather than separations from or usurpations of the body. While a properly motivated renewal movement is not the church and seeks to keep that very clear, it is a vital part of the church and functions in order to make the church more whole and more effectual.[11]

Much like the Restorationist movement represented by Robert Fife, the Church of God movement (Anderson) has been sensitive to the damage done to the church and its mission by denominational divisions when such divisions take to themselves the prerogatives belonging only to the whole body. It has thought of itself as a "movement" in Fife's terms, functioning at God's call *within* the body and *for* the body. Too often, however, even this unity movement has managed to facilitate awkward separations, in spite of itself.

A movement can facilitate the internal dialogue of the church only as it engages actively with the church, not when it retreats within its own confines out of self-preoccupation or fear of contamination by the beliefs and practices of other Christian traditions. A "movement" can

---

[11]Rex Koivisto attributes such wholesome characteristics to "denominations" (*One Lord, One Faith*, 102ff). Such groupings, he says, are inevitable sociologically. Even people uniting around a non-denominational platform are not thereby kept from potentially being at least part of what they oppose (102). Koivisto quotes Wolfhart Pannenberg: "The mutual relationship of the various regional or denominational traditions within the one Christian world should be thought of in terms of that type of multiplicity of concrete forms in which the catholic fullness of the church comes to expression. The multiplicity of such traditions in church order, doctrine, and liturgy does not exclude catholicity as long as each of them holds itself open, beyond its own distinctive features, for the Christian rights of the others and feels a responsibility, not just for its own tradition, but for the whole of Christian history and its heritage" (104). Similarly: "A monolithic denomination is not desirable. In Christian history, revival times have often occasioned a new order in Roman Catholicism or a new denomination in Protestantism—not mergers. . . . The Church can be one and apostolic and catholic right while it exists in denominational forms" (J. Kenneth Grider, *A Wesleyan-Holiness Theology*, 484-485).

176

destroy its own genius by failing to move creatively within the larger body. Lutheranism, for instance, has sought to avoid this trap by thinking of its own confessions of faith as an offer made to the larger church.[12] When, however, an offer moves to ultimatum, lacking appreciation for the valid offers of others, a movement becomes a "sect" in the negative sense.

Denominated bodies can be honorable and effective if they are not honored as ends in themselves, if they function cooperatively as patterns of partnership in relation to the whole body, and if they function as "movements" seeking to facilitate the health of the whole church. There is nothing inherently divisive in a group of Christians following the natural sociological process of "denominating" itself. In fact,

> no one form should be judged divisive just because it is a form. . . . Diversity is not division when the spirit of relating to those beyond the group is kept alive. . . . Diversity is one thing, while a spirit of division is quite another. . . . Every Christian has a legacy in every other Christian. We experience that legacy only as we receive each other and relate, moving eagerly beyond group boundaries.[13]

A helpful analogy was shared at the centennial consultation on the heritage of the Church of God movement.[14] The Gulf Stream is a marvelous movement of water that

---

[12]See E. Gritsch, R. Jenson, *Lutheranism: The Theological Movement and Its Confessional Writings* (Philadelphia: Fortress Press, 1976), chapter one. Carl Braaten speaks of Lutheranism much as the Church of God movement always has spoken of itself: "Lutheranism is not essentially a church but a movement.... It is a confessional movement that exists for the sake of reforming the whole church of Christ by the canon of the gospel. The. . .structures of Lutheranism are interim measures, ready to go out of business as soon as their provisional aims are realized" (*Principles of Lutheran Theology*, 46).

[13]James Earl Massey, *Concerning Christian Unity*, 75, 78, 82.

[14]This centennial consultation was convened in February, 1980, at the School of Theology of Anderson University, Anderson, Indiana. Note also the centennial celebration of the Church of God movement in

leaves the Gulf of Mexico and flows as a warming river across the vast expanse of the Atlantic Ocean to the European continent. The general path of the warmer water is obvious. Its influence on the ocean environment is definite as it moves along. But its boundaries are imprecise. It is open to all the surrounding ocean, influencing and being influenced. T. Franklin Miller judged this an appropriate image of what a movement should be like within the larger body of Christ. The opposite, by whatever name, tries delivering its water to Europe in a sealed pipeline, neither warming nor being enriched by the much larger body on the way. The opposite of a movement (an isolated "sect") thinks it knows itself to be the true water without need of enrichment and not wishing to risk being chilled by outside contact.

Christian unity is both a gift of God and the achievement of those committed to its fullest realization. Diversity can be a source of freedom and creativity in the church, the opposite of a regimented and premature uniformity. The diamond of Christian truth has many facets. Difference is not bad unless it hardens into an arrogant, anti-catholic exclusiveness, or deviates from the biblical revelation that is to form the church in all of its expressions. Groupings of Christians need not represent an evil just because they exist as distinct groupings. The question is whether they are in conflict or communion, whether they are contributing to or detracting from the whole body of Christ. Bodies that cut themselves off are acting against the church, even if their divisive platforms include the call for Christian unity (an accusation sometimes leveled at the Church of God movement, particularly in its

---

Germany that occurred in Hamburg, Germany, September, 1994. A featured guest speaker was the director of the German Evangelical Alliance, an interdenominational Christian organization with which the Church of God movement in Germany had recently affiliated. Such affiliation expressed the desire to cooperate with, contribute to, and benefit from the larger church.

178

earliest decades).[15]

The church today is faced with a twin danger. Divisiveness, always tempting, is sinful in its unjustified pride and imperialism. Syncretism, however, often seeks to correct such narrowness by being willing "to do almost anything to gain an external unity" and in the process "is susceptible to mating with any ideological partner around, usually at the cost of loss of centered orthodoxy."[16] The challenge is to be "orthodox" and "radical," belonging to the mainstream of the Christian tradition, but in a distinctive, constructive, and renewing way.

Gabriel Fackre identifies two ideological partners, new "tribes" that sometimes function today like the old sects in a negative, cut-off way. One is an "imperial tribalism" that rallies around the modernist assumption that truth comes by right knowledge and exists to make this world more livable. Since knowledge is thought to root in historical circumstance and vested interest, it is said that one knows true Christian identity only when one acts on behalf of the oppressed. The *doer* is the *knower*. Truth is tribally defined since it is restricted to those involved in the prescribed way. The other is "confessional tribalism" that

---

[15]In one sense the church is called to be "sectarian." When it is the eschatological church born of the Pentecostal vision, carrying the distinctive marks, and exercising the distinctive gifts of the Spirit, the church moves toward the "sect" type of ecclesiology described by Ernst Troeltsch (*The Social Teaching of the Christian Churches*, 1912). He describes Christianity as having three organizational orientations, church, sect, and mysticism. Books like Stanley Hauerwas and William Willimon, *Resident Aliens* (Nashville: Abingdon Press, 1989) and the whole Believers' Church tradition call for a distinctive, counter-cultural identity as the authentic way of really being the church in our kind of world. In another sense, however, the church should resist sectarianism. "The Disciples of Christ and the Church of God (Anderson, Indiana) have witnessed long and loud about the need to heal the divisions within Christendom, advising that rules and opinions not found in Scripture are injurious to fellowship and the experience of unity. The intent has been to help the rest of the churches become aware of how denominational separatism limits fellowship and hinders having a visible unity" (James Earl Massey, *Concerning Christian Unity*, 90).

[16]Thomas Oden, *Life in the Spirit*, 313.

knows no final truth, "only illusory claims and interest-laden agendas ripe for deconstruction." In this instance it is assumed that one "can never find 'the truth'; one must be content with what one has, not things truthful but things meaningful." Our tribe is our tribe with our distinctive language, lore, and codes. While live-and-let-live is the prevailing attitude, there is "border control" that maintains meaningful identity. These two tribal ideologies both threaten a unified church, one by arrogance, the other by apathy.[17]

Organizational variety in the church appears inevitable as Christians of varying backgrounds focus their lives around differing concerns in order to advance varying understandings of the gospel in multiple cultures. The problem is not the variety as such, but rigid spirits of exclusiveness that act *against* and not *with* and *for* the whole church. The problem of division is its unjustified exclusivism (a sign to the world that is injurious to Christ's mission). Ignoring the necessary mark of catholicity, a divisive body falsely expands some insight, gift, or group tradition into a restricting dominance, failing to hear that "the eye cannot say to the hand, 'I have no need of you.' . . . If the whole body were an eye, where would the hearing be?" (1 Cor. 12:21, 17). True division makes human experience normative, even when insisting on Scriptural authority, since only the official and humanly conditioned reading of the particular "tribe" is judged acceptable by that tribe.

The goal of Christian unity, possible in the midst of diversity by the work of the one Spirit, is commitment to the one Lord who is head of the one church. Such Christ-centered unity is not a matter of creedal uniformity, but consists of communication between Christian groups, the mutual enrichment by varying traditions, with the standard of the faith, Jesus Christ, the exclusive possession of

---

[17]Gabriel Fackre, *Ecumenical Faith in Evangelical Perspective*, 74-76, 85.

no one group. "The fullness of the gospel proclaimed in the church," concludes Gabriel Fackre, "will be in direct proportion to the mutual correction and completion of the church's tribal monologues. Let the imperialist who raids and the confessionalist who patrols dismantle their juggernauts and take down their barricades."[18]

The hope is not for a uniformity with all distinctives somehow eliminated. Christians are to be reconciled *in their diversity*. Observing that real differences already existed even in the early church, Thomas Oden insists that "genuine unity in the whole body of Christ is not merely a matter of improved organizational management. It is a unity enabled by the Spirit that awakens legitimate diversity without imposing premature uniformity."[19] Being together in Christ by the Spirit is to be "catholic." Being in touch with one's own traditional distinctives within the Christian family, while remaining open to the wisdom resident in the larger reality of the church, is to be "radical" in a divinely-intended sense. The Church of God movement (Anderson) has hoped in this way to be "free-church catholic," a healing and uniting force within the whole body of Christ.

There is to be a careful juxtaposition of unity and diversity, both kept focused and constructive by a divine enablement that incites the wakefulness of Christians and resists efforts at human domestication of others or of God's work. John Frame joins the tradition of the Church of God movement in calling for "ecclesiastical revolutionaries," Christians willing to yield themselves and their status-quo tribal instincts for the sake of the higher calling of God to the church.[20]

---

[18]Ibid., 86. Down should come all denominational chauvinisms that promote the interests of one Christian body over against and at the expense of others. The concern always should be for the health of the whole body of Christ.

[19]Thomas Oden, *Life in the Spirit*, 311.

[20]John Frame, *Evangelical Reunion*, 16.

The church is God's. The church is one. As the holy, catholic, apostolic body of Christ, it is to be a sign to the world of the already coming Kingdom. How is it to be such a sign? The church, a *holy* community in an unholy world, a *united* community of faith in a divided world of unfaith, is to be an active agent of *reconciliation* and *peace*.

Appendix G

CONDENSATION OF "EXPERIENCE" IN TWO CHURCH TRADITIONS: DIFFERING SEMANTIC WORLDS[1]

by
Byron C. Lambert, 1994

In philosophy, empiricism is an epistemological theory defined in opposition to rationalism. In the early modern age it arose in reaction to the metaphysics of Descartes (1596-1650), Leibniz (1646-1716), and Spinoza (1632-1677), who sought to bind the whole of reality together, including God, by deduction from one or two fundamental principles. The rationalists believed that the universe was best approached and understood along the lines of a logical system, whatever the five outer senses might lead humans to believe.

A science of nature was growing, however, which looked to the outer world of sense experience as a guide to what

---

[1] In recent years the Church of God movement (Anderson) and the Christian Churches/Churches of Christ have been in dialogue, each seeking to understand better the other tradition for the sake of enhancing Christian unity and mission. The first group, a holiness body rooted in American revivalism, has had a particular understanding of the nature and role of Christian "experience." It differs at least in subtle ways from the understanding typical of the second group. In a dialogue session in October, 1994, Dr. Byron Lambert, representing the latter body, presented this essay in hope of furthering mutual understanding of this crucial subject. It subsequently was published in the *Wesleyan Theological Journal* (30:1, Spring 1995) and is reproduced here in condensed form with permission of the *Journal*.

reality is truly like. Francis Bacon (1561-1626) was one of the first to formulate and make popular the new approach. Comparing the studies of metaphysicians unfavorably to that of spiders spinning theories out of their bellies, Bacon said philosophers should rather use the bee as a model, collect data from everyday experience, sort it out in concert with one another, conduct experiments, and learn nature's secrets by organized observation of her regularities.

Locke held that the mind was awakened solely by the action of the senses. Pushed to the extreme, such an approach would hold that everything we know is limited to what the experience of the senses delivers. In its more moderate form, such an approach would only say that the materials for knowledge are sense-based. Locke was an empiricist in the latter sense, but the logic of his theory was carried to radical extremes by Berkeley and Hume.

What has to be remembered is that Locke was not just an epistemological empiricist; he was also a rationalist. He was not a rationalist after the fashion of the Continental thinkers, however. Locke used experience-governed thought, not to build a complex ontology, but as a method of reining in irrationalism, hallucination, and superstition at the popular level. He also warned against imagining that the human mind has unlimited powers of knowledge and said that, for life's ultimate meanings and purposes, human beings have to depend on divine revelation.

Empiricism is a philosophical theory, or way of looking at things, which can be stretched in more than one direction. Both the Christian Churches/Churches of Christ and the Church of God movement (Anderson) belong philosophically to the British Empiricist tradition, but they have understood experience in somewhat different ways. Alexander Campbell (1788-1866) and John Wesley (1703-1791) both took the Lockean analysis of knowledge as a given, but went in contrasting directions in their use of it.[2]

---

[2]Good, but brief discussions of the Lockeanism of Campbell and Wesley can be found in Leroy Garrett, *The Stone-Campbell Movement: An Anecdotal History of Three Churches* (Joplin, MO: College Press, 1981),

Neither accepted the further developments of empiricism by Berkeley and Hume, preferring the more widely disseminated and enduring opinions of the great originator of the philosophy.

For Campbell and his co-laborers, experience, as a test of fact, was what is publicly verifiable. When they spoke of Christian experience they referred primarily to what had happened in gospel history, as verified by faithful witnesses in Scripture. The faith of the Christian was to be based on the apostolic experience, since it alone could be reliably certified as revelation. While "Christian experience" as an expression necessarily includes what happens to Christian people as they live out their spiritual development in all times and places, these multitudinous personal experiences, each private and particular, for Restorationists are hardly the test for truths that must serve the church as a whole and universally. It is normative, not clinical experience which must serve to unite the church.

Christian Church/Church of Christ people, therefore, tend to have little regard for subjectivity, as such, in religion. If they speak of their "religious experiences," they do so diffidently, thinking of God's answers to prayer, unusual providences, or the work of the Holy Spirit in their lives as phenomena understood best at a distance and in retrospect. Almost all of their enthusiasm centers around the notions of belief, correct understanding, and

---

29-35, and Colin W. Williams, *John Wesley's Theology Today* (New York: Abingdon Press, 1960), 31. Some Christian Churches/Churches of Christ leaders like Dean E. Walker, however, believe Campbell was more in the tradition of Thomas Reid (1710-1796) and Common Sense philosophy. See Walker, *Adventuring for Christian Unity and Other Essays*, collected and arranged by Thomas Foust and edited by William Richardson (Johnson City, TN: Emmanuel School of Religion, 1992), 446. Walker's revisionism may stem from his opposition to the Lockeanism of liberals in the Disciples movement like Edward Scribner Ames (1870-1958). For a discussion of Ames, see D. Newell Williams, ed., *A Case Study of Mainstream Protestantism: the Disciples' Relation to American Culture*, 1880-1989 (Grand Rapids: Eerdmans, and St. Louis: Chalice Press, 1991), 120-125.

obedience. Terms like loyalty ("our loyal brethren"), faith-fulness to Scripture, joy of duty done, satisfaction with things being worked out according to Divine plan, seeing the deeper meanings in Christ's words or those of the apostles, define what they mean by "Christian experi-ence."

In the last generation there has been a growing empha-sis on the inward workings of the Holy Spirit, but it is a sanctification doctrine entirely gradualist in its approach. Attempts to bring "deeper life" studies into the life of Christian Church/Church of Christ people have met with only marginal success. Expressions like "God told me to do thus and so," or "I felt irresistibly moved in this direction by the Holy Spirit," or "God laid it on my heart to tell you this" are met with suspicion, if not outright rejection. Restorationists do not hold testimony meetings.

All of this does not mean that the people of Restorationist churches are unemotional. They weep when believers come forward in their services to accept Christ; they enjoy music, poetry, choruses, and sermons that excite the heart and deepen commitment; but these are expressions that fix loyalties previously entered into men-tally and volitionally. They do not weep in order to be saved, but because they are saved.

The people of the Wesleyan tradition, including the Church of God, tend to struggle with assurance of the quality of their Christian commitment; the Restorationist struggles with the initial commitment itself, as the defin-ing act of Christian birth. The former wants to feel that he or she has gone through the proper exercise; the latter considers only that a decision needs to be made and main-tained. The Restorationist too often is thought of as a rationalist, but is better described as a volitionist, not typ-ically intellectualist, but a pragmatist, a doer, one who looks for results. Christian "experience" for such believers is primarily found in success in a congregation's numerical growth, faithful giving, a respectable missionary budget, an efficient church staff, excitement in the fellowship gatherings, and the quiet joy of prayer circles and Bible studies.

Obviously, there is much of Locke's genteel rationalism embedded in the thought patterns of early Restorationists, but it is not so much the epistemology of the *Essay Concerning Human Understanding* as the style of thinking found in *The Reasonableness of Christianity* and his commentary on Galatians. Locke's fundamental picture of the human mind works its way into the latter works, since they presuppose the limitation of human knowledge, the need for specific revelation, and the vanity of dogmatizing. For Locke there are only a few majestic truths God asks us to believe. For example, he says that the four Gospels have only one purpose, that of showing Jesus to be the Messiah and Saviour of the world. Walter Scott's *Messiahship* (1859) is only a descant on this theme.

Historically, the emotions calling the Stone-Campbell movement into existence were strikingly different from those giving rise to the Church of God (Anderson) holiness movement. The Campbells and company were distressed at the uncharitable and wasteful divisions among Presbyterians, and then by extension the many more numerous divisions in Christendom. Their solution—one they thought the New World had been called into existence to support—was simple: return to the universally accepted word of the New Testament, abandoning all those post-apostolic institutions and tests of orthodoxy that clutter and clog church history, and allowing to reappear the fundamental unity of the church that lay concealed under it all. The plan was rational, simple, and Scriptural. It is easy to see that the roots of Restorationism sink deep into the eighteenth century. In many ways it would be possible to see the Stone-Campbell movement as an eighteenth century movement in assumptions and style, one working its way through the nineteenth and twentieth centuries—albeit with increasing difficulty.

The historical circumstance of John Wesley was both similar and different. On May 24, 1738, at 8:45 in the evening, at a Moravian meeting in Aldersgate near London where a reading of Luther's commentary on Romans was in progress, John Wesley felt his heart "strangely warmed" by an assurance that his sins were forgiven. He had been baptized as an infant in the Anglican church, brought up in a priestly home, accepted the teaching of all the *Thirty-Nine Articles,* was ordained as a presbyter in 1728, sent as a missionary to Georgia, had gathered around himself at Oxford a small group of believers who were seeking to reach new levels of Christian devotion and purity ("the Holiness Club"), and had steeped himself in the devotional literature of Thomas à Kempis, William Law, and Jeremy Taylor. But he was still dissatisfied with his Christian experience. On his way to America, Wesley had been struck by the calmness of certain Moravians on shipboard during a storm and, in a conversation with one of them, Peter Böhler, was questioned about the adequacy of his Christian faith: "Have you the witness within yourself?" Böhler asked. "Does the Spirit of God bear witness with your spirit that you are a child of God?"

Wesley had never had the question put just that way. Conversion, real conversion, was what the 18th-century church had lacked. The whole upper class in England appeared lost to unbelief, a lostness that threatened to spread to the rest of society. The church was largely latitudinarian; immorality in the streets and on the stage seemed out of control. Yet all these citizens, listed in church baptismal registries, were supposed to be Christian. But they had no "living experience" of their religion. They needed a conscious awakening to Christ's power for their lives. What they needed was Wesley's experience to be theirs.

In January of 1738 Wesley wrote in his journal, "I want that faith which none can have without knowing that he hath it." It was the tangible, palpable work of the Holy Spirit in his heart, directly recognized inwardly, at once and infallibly, that validated all he had previously believed and hoped. The truth of Christ now had "the living sense" which the apostles of the first century had written about; he believed he now had the assurance of salvation they spoke of. The experience was self- authenticating. Perhaps it could be argued that Wesley's experience is anything but empiricist in the usual sense, since it transcends sensory knowledge and is not subject to public test. Wesley extends Locke's doctrine in a new direction:

> [S]eeing our ideas are not innate, but must all originally come from our senses, which in this respect profit nothing, as being altogether incapable of discerning objects of this kind: Not those only that are called natural senses, which in this respect profit nothing, as being altogether incapable of discerning objects of a spiritual kind; but spiritual senses, exercised to discern spiritual good and evil. It is necessary that you have the hearing ear, and the seeing eye, emphatically so called, that you have a new class of senses opened in your soul, not depending on organs of flesh and blood. . . . The ideas of faith differ toto genere from those of external sensation. . . . What a gulf is here! By what art will reason get over the immense chasm? This cannot be, till the Almighty come in to your succor, and give you that faith you have hitherto despised. Then upborne, as it were, on eagle's wings, you shall soar away into the regions of eternity; and your enlightened reason shall explore even "the deep things of God"; God himself "revealing them to you by his Spirit."[3]

What I am trying to do is show that there is an empiricism of the heart, that it seems as perfectly plausible as that of the head, that it can be based as surely on Locke as the empiricism of the senses. The thing that it does, however, is overturn Locke's particular sort of rationalism. What is not evident in Wesley is the cool, genteel rationalism of Locke's "reasonable" Christianity. While there is certainly a turning away from traditional conventions and

---

[3]As quoted in Thomas Jackson, ed., *The Works of John Wesley, A.M.*, 14 vols., 3rd ed. (London: John Mason, 1829), 8:13.

established authority, there is no appetite in Neo-Augustinian terms, for the rare power of simple ideas, cogently expressed. In a comparison between Wesley and Alexander Campbell, it is Campbell who is the Neo-Augustinian, non-experience centered empiricist (if the paradox can be permitted), and Wesley, who carries Lockeanism in religion to its ultimate expression. Let Maximum Piette say it again for Wesley: the rebirth in the Holy Spirit puts the believer in a new universe. Like the new infant, suddenly the convert has an awareness of God, new spiritual senses to see good and evil, "sees" what it is to be loved and pardoned by God, can now "hear" and "obey," "knows" joy and peace, "dwells" in God.[4]

It is "the experience" itself which places the Church of God movement squarely in the empiricist tradition by way of John Wesley as his heritage evolved in revivalistic America. This is confirmed in the paper "Defining the Vision: a Heritage to Cherish" delivered by church historian Merle Strege at the annual meeting of the Indiana Ministries of the Church of God, September, 1993. In section 2.5 of his paper, titled "The Church is Experientially Grounded," he states that the Church of God movement holds that "the church [is] a place where the experience of salvation makes one a member." He traces this emphasis to the Pietistic roots which feed the epistemology of the Church of God movement. "Knowing God" and being "certain" of one's salvation are phrases springing from such an epistemology. Strege states that the fundamental notion that "we 'know' by way of experience" allows Church of God people to alter their traditional doctrine if it needs to be brought "into conformity with new insights derived from experience." He cites as an example this movement's belief about divine healing which has undergone modification through the experience of "new light." He notes that it is this doctrine of experience which grounds the move-

---

[4]Maximum Piette, *John Wesley in the Evolution of Protestantism*, trans. J.B. Howard (London: Sheed and Ward, 1938), 440.

ment's opposition to creeds, since creeds represent "a spurious substitution of the Spirit by the letter." He says, Church of God folk rally around Christ "experientially."

I see nothing in most of this to which Christian Churches/Churches of Christ people would not give a hearty "Amen." It is possible that the Christian Churches/Churches of Christ emphasizes conceptual study a tad more than the Church of God. We, too, judge God to be at work in ourselves individually and through the Church, although we might be wary of saying "We sense Him at work," which seems to imply an immediate awareness of His working at the moment. We prefer to be less hasty and more retrospective, waiting to see whether present experiences really deliver what we hope.

Church of God theologian Kenneth Jones responded to my inquiry in a letter dated June 25, 1994. He confessed that he had been frustrated in trying to explain what a religious experience is in itself, since he and a few others with whom he had shared my questions found it incomprehensible that a Christian could be converted without experiencing it. He was careful to point out that what the Church of God teaches is not a form of rootless, revelationless mysticism, that religious experiences of whatever sort are not "a source of truth or knowledge," and that Scripture is the only guide to knowing if one is saved: "Experience must always be tested by the Word." There might be other confirmatory sources of truth like tradition, reason, and experience, but they are secondary, according to Jones.[5] The Church of God, he says, rejects both Schleiermacher and Pentecostalism. Too much can be read into Wesley's phrase that "experience is self-authenticating," he continues; the "experience" is entirely fictitious if obedience and holiness of life do not follow it. "Being saved" means that God has accepted that person into the church. Again, there is very little in the views of

---

[5]See Donald A.D. Thorsen, *The Wesleyan Quadrilateral: Scripture, Tradition, Reason & Experience as a Model of Evangelical Theology* (Grand Rapids: Zondervan, 1990).

Jones that sounds contrary to the Christian Churches/
Churches of Christ understanding of Scripture.

The value of this investigation may simply be that of
calling attention to those factors that govern the somewhat differing ways that the Christian Churches/
Churches of Christ and the Church of God movement have
looked at Christian unity, thus showing that presupposi-
tional or worldview influences on theology may have more
to do with barriers to our overt unity in Christ than any
doctrines we espouse in our more visible teaching agenda.
It is important that we reexamine those presuppositions
controlling our Christian perspectives. Certainly,
Christian Churches/Churches of Christ have some listening to do when it comes to Church of God teaching on the
Holy Spirit. We have not brought our thinking up to date
with the actual language of the New Testament when it
comes to the indwelling of the Spirit. It is encouraging to
see Restorationists take more interest in pneumatology, in
the topic of baptism with the Holy Spirit, and with
empowerment doctrines contained in neglected Scriptures
like Acts 4:31 (where the whole assembly was "filled" with
the Holy Spirit after receiving the "gift" in Acts 2:38),
Rom. 8:9-11, 16 (the Spirit lives in ordinary Christians
and "testifies" inwardly), 1 Cor. 2:12 (the Spirit is given to
us so "that we may understand what God has freely given
us"), Gal. 4:6 (it is the Spirit who calls out, "Abba," in our
hearts), Col. 1:27 (Christ in us is the hope of glory), all of
this over and above letting the word of Christ dwell in us
as we teach and sing to each other (Col. 3:16), 1 John
3:24b (where we know Christ lives in us "by the Spirit he
gave us"), and other like passages.

The Church of God movement can make us stay open
to those previously opaque and mysterious Scriptures
which speak of the vital presence of the Holy Spirit in our
personal lives and in the counsel of the gathered faithful.
If we listen, we shall be far ahead of where we are now
and might possibly understand where we have failed in
our restorative mission to the Church. In the same way, by

remaining open to their principle of listening to the voice of the Spirit in the church as they seek to understand Scripture, the Church of God may find that the mystical attaches to more than the psychological, that there is more to "spirit" than just mental factors, and that there are profoundly non-cognitive elements at work in the first (and second) century "whole person" understanding of salvation. I speak here of the sacramental aspects of prime Christianity, misunderstood by both Christian Churches/ Churches of Christ and the Church of God as either legal or optional attachments to faith. The more I investigate early Christian thinking about the relation between body and spirit, the material and the volitional, the corporate and the individual, the more convinced I am that we have never entered into the worldview of the first church and understood its notion of whole-universe redemption. I think we are more prisoners of the Cartesian universe than we have realized.

Both of these movements, in their divergent empiricisms, are nevertheless pervasively ahistorical. Both miss what is instructive in church tradition. They find it difficult to account for the church between A.D. 100 and either 1812 (the Brush Run Church) or 1881 (D.S. Warner and the *Gospel Trumpet*) and experience a deep disconnection with historical Christendom (something very unlike John Wesley, the Anglican). Being anti-creedal, anti-hierarchical, and anti-liturgical, both movements have all the difficulties associated with starting over again, with its cost in theological naivety and ecclesiastical bumbling (the Church of God less so in this latter respect). The Christian Churches/Churches of Christ have the great added cost of their recent separation from the Disciples, with the loss of most of those institutions antedating the division.

I confess to a certain joyful mystification over the results of independent missions around the world and church planting at home, occasions in which God has worked through the massive incohesiveness of so much that we do. Still, our tendencies to hyper-congregationalism and whimsical individualism keep us from having much of a "presence" vis-à-vis the world we are trying to save and the Church we are trying to unite.

Appendix H

THE FAITH AND ORDER MOVEMENT: HOLINESS CHURCH PARTICIPATION[1]

by
Gilbert W. Stafford, 1997

The phrases "holiness movement," "ecumenical movement," and "charismatic movement" are widely used in general conversation. They evoke responses of allegiance and/or concern. The "faith and order movement," however, is a subject not widely used in general conversation and therefore may evoke little more than a blank stare. It is a movement of significance to contemporary Christianity and one to which bodies associated with the "holiness" tradition should give increasing attention.

The Genesis and History of Faith and Order

The genesis of the Faith and Order movement can be traced to an event that took place at the 1910 World Missionary Conference held in Edinburgh, Scotland. There, for the first time since the rise of denominational

---

[1]This essay by Gilbert Stafford of Anderson University also appears in the *Wesleyan Theological Journal* (32:1, Spring 1997). Used here by permission. Since 1984 Dr. Stafford has represented the Commission on Christian Unity of the Church of God (Anderson) at Faith and Order meetings.

Christianity, a world conference was held with participants who were not simply those interested in the subject matter, but persons officially chosen by denominations and missionary societies. Those at Edinburgh had the responsibility of representing the positions and concerns of their ecclesial sponsors. This put a different stamp on the character of this conference. It was first and foremost an officially representative gathering.

In the course of the conference it became apparent, at least to some, that the identities imposed on emerging churches around the world were the result of theological and doctrinal disagreements having historical roots and social contexts that were foreign to the newer churches. These various denominational identities, therefore, did not reflect their own wrestling with faith issues. This was of such great concern to Bishop Charles H. Brent of the Protestant Episcopal Church in the United States—at the time Bishop of the Philippine Islands—that near the end of the Edinburgh meeting he pled for the churches in the future to convene for the purpose of addressing not only missionary concerns but doctrinal concerns as well.

After Edinburgh, Brent did what he could in his own church to bring this about. In October of that year—on the day prior to the convening of the General Convention of the Protestant Episcopal Church in Cincinnati, Ohio—Brent addressed a mass meeting of Episcopalians. He shared his passionate concern that the churches begin addressing doctrinal issues—i.e., matters of faith and order—in formalized discussions between persons officially chosen by their respective communions to represent them. On October 19, 1910, the Episcopal church responded by passing unanimously the following resolution:

> That a Joint Commission be appointed to bring about a Conference for the consideration of questions touching Faith and Order, and that all Christian Communions throughout the world which confess Our Lord Jesus

Christ as God and Saviour be asked to unite with us in arranging for and conducting such a Conference.[2]

The vision was caught by other churches and in 1911 the proposal for such a conference was communicated in a letter to Christian communions around the world.[3] While the response was positive, the intricacies of planning such a gathering and the turmoil associated with World War I slowed down the process. Finally, though, the first World Conference on Faith and Order was held in Lausanne, Switzerland, in 1927 with 394 delegates representing 108 churches from around the world. Subsequent conferences were held in Edinburgh (1937),[4] Lund, Sweden (1952),[5] Montreal, Canada (1963),[6] and Santiago de Compostela, Spain (1993).[7]

Besides the Missionary Conference movement and the Faith and Order movement, a third development, called the Life and Work movement, also emerged. Bishop Nathan Söderblom of Sweden was convinced that contemporary international and societal issues could be

---

[2]Tissington Tatlow, "The World Conference on Faith and Order," *A History of the Ecumenical Movement 1517-1948*, Fourth Edition, ed. Ruth Rouse and Stephen C. Neill, Vol. I of *A History of the Ecumenical Movement 1517-1968* (Geneva, Switz.: World Council of Churches, 1993), 407.

[3]Ibid., 420. For conference papers, proceedings, decisions, and membership, see H.N. Bate (ed.), *Faith and Order: Proceedings of the World Conference, Lausanne, August 3-21, 1927* (New York: Doran, 1927).

[4]See Leonard Hodgson, ed., *The Second World Conference on Faith and Order Held at Edinburgh, August 3-18, 1937* (London: Student Christian Movement Press, 1938).

[5]See Oliver S. Tomkins (ed.), *The Third Conference on Faith and Order Held at Lund, August 15th to 28th, 1952* (London: SCM, 1953).

[6]See P.C. Rodger and Lukas Vischer (ed.), *The Fourth World Conference on Faith and Order, Montreal, 1963* (New York: Association Press, 1964).

[7]See Thomas F. Best and Günther Gassmann (ed.), *Official Report of the Fifth World Conference on Faith and Order: On the Way to Fuller Koinonia* (Geneva, Switz.: WCC Publications, 1994). Also, Günther Gassmann (ed.), *Documentary History of Faith and Order, 1963-1993* (Geneva, Switz.: WCC Publications, 1993).

addressed adequately only by a Christian church united for social witness. The view held was that, whereas doctrine inevitably divides, social witness can be an opportunity for a united Christianity. On the basis of these strong convictions, the Universal Christian Conference on Life and Work was convened in Stockholm, Sweden, in 1925, and the second conference was held in Oxford, England, in 1937.

By this time, however, there was a growing realization that life-and-work was inevitably theological, and, consequently, could not be kept in isolation from faith-and-order considerations. In 1937, with Life and Work meeting in Scotland, and Faith and Order meeting in England, it was convenient for the two to consider working as one unit. The decision was made to formalize the union of the two movements, to be known jointly as the World Council of Churches. The chaos of World War II, however, kept this process from coming to culmination until 1948 when the WCC held its founding Assembly in Amsterdam, Holland.[8]

With the union of Faith and Order and Life and Work, the latter ceased to exist as a separate entity whereas Faith and Order continued as a distinctive movement which, while now sponsored by the WCC, continued to be wider than WCC membership.

The Holiness Presence in Faith And Order

No representative from an American Holiness church was present at Lausanne, Edinburgh, or Lund. The first Holiness participation was at Montreal in 1963 with a delegate (Gene W. Newberry) and two observers (Louis Meyer and John W.V. Smith) from the Church of God (Anderson),[9] and with two U.S.A. delegates from the Salvation Army (Commissioner S. Hepburn and Lt-Col.

---

[8]All three streams finally came together when in 1961 the International Missionary Council merged with the WCC at New Delhi, India.

[9]Rodger and Vischer, *Fourth World Conference*, 107.

P.S. Kaiser).[10] At Santiago de Compostela in 1993, Holiness representatives included Cheryl Bridges-Johns of the Church of God (Cleveland)[11] and Susie C. Stanley of the Church of God (Anderson).[12]

In 1957 Faith and Order sponsored a conference particularly for the church in the United States and Canada. Called the North American Conference on Faith and Order, it was held September 3-10 of that year in Oberlin, Ohio. Regarding Holiness participation, the Salvation Army was a full member with two representatives. One was a member of the study section on "Authority and Freedom in Church Government," and the other in the section on "Racial and Economic Stratification."[13] In addition to this, the Holiness movement was indirectly represented by James Royster of the Church of God (Anderson) who was a youth delegate from the Interseminary Movement.[14] Consultants from churches that were not members of the World Council included Donald Demaray from the Free Methodist Church, who worked in the section on "Baptism Into Christ,"[15] and John W. V. Smith from the Church of God (Anderson) who worked in the section on "Doctrinal Consensus and Conflict."[16] In addition, observers—a category for those who, while not official delegates of the sending churches, could nevertheless participate—included three from the Church of God (Anderson): Clarence W. Hatch who worked in the study section on "Authority and Freedom in Church Government,"[17] Gene W. Newberry who worked in the section on

---

[10]Ibid., 115.

[11]Best and Gassmann, *Fifth World Conference*, xx.

[12]Ibid., xxii.

[13]Paul S. Minear (ed.), *The Nature of the Unity We Seek: Official Report of the North American Conference on Faith and Order, September 3-10, 1957, Oberlin, Ohio* (St. Louis: Bethany, 1958), 295.

[14]Ibid., 296.

[15]Ibid., 297.

[16]Ibid., 298.

[17]Ibid., 299.

"The Life of the Congregation,"[18] and Harold L. Phillips in the section on "Imperatives and Motivations."[19]

Ever since Oberlin the Church of God (Anderson) has continued to participate. Serving as commissioner until his death in 1984 was John W. V. Smith, and for a short time in 1983-84 Juanita Lewis, and since 1984, Gilbert W. Stafford. The only other Holiness church (though also Pentecostal) that currently participates is the Church of God (Cleveland) represented by Cheryl Bridges-Johns. Two additional Holiness churches participate indirectly by virtue of the Wesleyan Theological Society's appointment of Paul Bassett of the Church of the Nazarene and Donald Dayton of the Wesleyan Church. WTS participation began in 1985 with the appointment of Dayton and David Cubie of the Church of the Nazarene. Bassett followed Cubie in 1988. The Church of God (Anderson) is, therefore, the only non-Pentecostal Holiness church that participates officially as a church.

Faith and Order work in the United States is now sponsored by the National Council of the Churches of Christ in the U.S.A. (NCCC). In keeping with the long-standing tradition of including churches that are not members of the NCCC, present membership encompasses a wide range of non-NCCC churches, including Roman Catholic, Church of God (Cleveland, TN), Church of God in Christ, Mennonite, Friends General Conference, International Evangelical Church, Lutheran Church—Missouri Synod, Independent Christian Churches, Assemblies of God, Christian Reformed, Cooperative Baptist Fellowship, Korean Presbyterian, Churches of Christ (non-instrumental), and the Church of God (Anderson).

The Ongoing Vision of Faith and Order

In my twelve years of Faith and Order work, I have found that the original purposes of the movement are still in place:

[18]Ibid., 300.
[19]Ibid.

To proclaim the essential oneness of the Church of Christ and to keep prominently before . . . the churches the obligation to manifest that unity and its urgency for the work of evangelism.

To study questions of faith, order, and worship with the relevant social, cultural, political, racial and other factors in their bearing on the unity of the Church. . . .

To study matters in the present relationships of the churches to one another which cause difficulties and need theological clarification. . . .[20]

What Samuel McCrea Cavert said in 1970 about Faith and Order is still true:

The Faith and Order movement, in both its worldwide and its national aspects, has consistently adhered to the policy of making its contribution through study and dialogue. It has carefully refrained from presenting any particular plan of union, regarding this as necessarily the responsibility of the ecclesiastical bodies themselves.[21]

The inaugural report of the 1996-1999 quadrennium of study states the current vision of Faith and Order in North America:

To further the longstanding work of Faith and Order on theological issues that are church-dividing and church-uniting by engaging more fully and directly the faithful people of the churches of Christ in ecclesial settings of ongoing worship and witness, with renewed commitment to engagement with churches in wide ranging ecclesial traditions, and thereby to nurture the NCCC's commitment to fuller ecclesial fellowship.[22]

---

[20]Quoted from the original constitution of Faith and Order in Minear, *Nature of the Unity.*, 13.

[21]Samuel McCrea Cavert, *Church Cooperation and Unity in America* (New York: Friendship Press, 1970), 336f.

[22]"Conspectus of Study, 1996-1999," Faith and Order, The National Council of the Churches of Christ in the U.S.A. (distributed at Pasadena, CA: Fuller Theological Seminary, March 15-16), 2.

The Benefits of Participating in Faith and Order

What, then, are the benefits of a church's participation in Faith and Order? I list the following nine benefits.

1. Participation is **an opportunity to learn *about* other traditions in a dialogical setting**. One of the more rewarding intellectual experiences of my life was my subgroup's discussion in an earlier triennium (as it was then) of our several understandings of apostolic faith. The fact that each Christian tradition makes claims of being apostolic in its faith provided a basis for vigorous discussion. In our extended deliberations we learned enough about each other's traditions to be able to identify points both of agreement and of divergence. We came to appreciate that all of us agree that being a church of apostolic faith includes at least these basic components: the confession that Jesus Christ is God and Savior; the guidance and inspiration of the Holy Spirit; the authoritative witness of the Scriptures; and the church as the community of faithful worship, witness, and service in the world. But we differ when it comes to other characteristics of what it means to be apostolic. Some traditions emphasize normative creedal and confessional statements; others emphasize normative teaching offices and polities; and others emphasize normative experiences of conversion, sanctification, holiness, and liberation.[23]

2. Faith and Order is an opportunity **to learn *from* other traditions**. Other traditions of the faith ask questions about one's own tradition that insiders tend not to ask. Once in a discussion about creeds, I explained that traditionally my own church (Church of God, Anderson) has been anti-creedalistic and that we even have a song, one stanza of which begins: "The day of sects and creeds for us forevermore is past."[24] "What!" an Orthodox priest

---

[23]See Thaddeus D. Horgan (ed.), *Apostolic Faith in America* (Grand Rapids: Eerdmans, 1988), 60-66.

[24]Charles W. Naylor, "The Church's Jubilee," *Worship the Lord: Hymnal of the Church of God* (Anderson: Warner Press, 1989), No. 312.

exclaimed, "how can you be Christian if you don't believe something?" He asked the right question and pressed the right issues for a tradition that has perhaps been too unreflective in its anti-creed rhetoric.

3. Faith and Order provides **an arena of discussion with a wide spectrum of Christian traditions**. This arena is wider than any other I know. Obviously, wide spectrums can be found in seminaries, theological forums, the academy, and in informal conversations. That which makes Faith and Order distinct from these, however, is that its members are, for the most part, chosen in some official way to represent their respective churches or organizations. In my case, I am elected by the Commission on Christian Unity of the Church of God, a commission made up both of representatives from our several national agencies and persons elected by the General Assembly of the Church of God.

The role of a participant is not that of setting forth his or her own personal theological positions, but those of the church being represented. Faith and Order participants are, in a sense, personifications of the differing traditions of Christian faith. For instance, when in my own subgroup Samuel Nafzger of the Lutheran Church—Missouri Synod speaks, we want him to give voice to the Missouri Synod. The assignment is not "Tell us what you personally think about this issue," but "Tell us, to the best of your ability, what you believe your church tradition holds concerning this matter." That goes even for the most overtly independent participants. When Doug Foster, a member of the Churches of Christ (non-instrumental), speaks, he, true to his tradition, makes it clear that he speaks only as Doug Foster, but we push him to represent to us, to the best of his ability, the Church of Christ tradition, not the Doug Foster view.

Where else can one find such a wide spectrum of thought being expressed by those who seek earnestly to speak for the respective traditions out of which they come? In my subgroup this quadrennium are representatives from churches as diverse as United Methodist, Orthodox, Roman Catholic, Churches of Christ (non-instrumental), Quaker, Evangelical Lutheran, Reformed Church in America, Assemblies of God, Presbyterian, United Church of Christ, National Baptist, and Church of God (Anderson).

4. Faith and Order provides each participant the opportunity **to teach other traditions about one's own tradition.** It is as though each tradition has the opportunity to bring other Christian traditions into its classroom for a short while for the purpose of teaching something about the Christian faith which it believes God has entrusted to it. Over the course of several years, for example, I have had the opportunity to present to my colleagues in Faith and Order several short papers: two on "The Apostolic Faith" as understood by the Church of God (Anderson), another titled "The Holy Spirit and the Experience of Church," and two papers on authority: "Authority in the Church of God (Anderson . . .)" and "Authorities for Making Decisions in the Church of God . . .". Also, I prepared a paper in answer to the question: "What would be the prerequisites for the Church of God (Anderson) to become a part of a Christian organization which is inclusive of Christian faith in its widest possible spectrum?" Another paper was prepared under the title, "Visioning for Koinonia in the Life of the Church." All of these were opportunities to teach others about matters which my church believes are crucial if the church at large is to be in health.

More recently, my papers have centered especially on our identification as a Holiness church. I presented a paper titled: "The Nineteenth Century Holiness Movement and Christian Unity." At the time of this writing, I am working with two other colleagues on presentations for an upcoming meeting in New Orleans. The first project has to do with "The Unitive Power of Holiness." The subgroup will consider my paper from the Holiness perspective and that of Father Kevin McMorrow, editor of

Ecumenical Trends, from the Roman Catholic perspective. Upon exchanging papers, each of us will write a response that will include three components: points of resonance with each other, differences, and points at which we simply do not understand the other. These four papers, then, will be presented to our subgroup for discussion.

The second project will use the same dialogical method on the subject of "The Hermeneutics of Reconciliation in Worship." My partner is John Erickson, professor of theology at St. Vladimir's Orthodox Theological Seminary in Crestwood, New York. In preparation for this assignment, Professor Erickson told me that since he had never worshipped in a Holiness church, he would like to have that experience. I put him in touch with a Church of God congregation which, without my knowing it, turned out to be close to St. Vladimir's. He has already worshiped there and has invited the Church of God to be guests at St. Vladimir's. In New Orleans, he and I will present our papers to the plenary, which we hope will be enriched both by Holiness and Orthodox insights.

5. Faith and Order work is the opportunity for one's own tradition to **recognize in other traditions dimensions of the apostolic faith which lie dormant in one's own.** While for one Christian tradition verbal confession about the person and work of Christ may be very much alive, an emphasis on the converting ministry of Christ in the here and now may lie dormant. In another tradition the enlivening presence of the Holy Spirit may be very much front and center, but the hard sayings about Kingdom life may lie dormant. For still another tradition an emphasis on personal conversion may be alive, but communal confession of the faith may be dormant. And for another tradition Kingdom teachings may be considered with great seriousness, but the joy of the risen Christ may be dormant. Faith and Order provides an ecclesial opportunity for each tradition of the faith to feed into the bloodstream of other traditions. It is in this kind of setting that the emphasis on personal sanctification, which Holiness

churches are convinced is part and parcel of the apostolic faith, can be fed into the bloodstream of a wide spectrum of other Christian traditions.

An example of how this happens is reflected in the following segment of the summary report of the last quadrennium:

> At Newark the Episcopal representative was inspired by what the Church of God (Anderson) representative had said about . . . join[ing] his church. When asked how people become members, he replied: "The process would be similar to the acceptance around this table. None of us has been formally 'checked out.' We sense some basic assumptions as we talk with each other. We share. It's not legalistic. . . ." As the representative of the Church of God (Cleveland) said in response to the information about the lack of formal joining in the Church of God (Anderson): "You are probably providing a model for the future, where things aren't so sharply defined as [they are] by organizational entities."[25]

Whether one agrees with the subject mentioned in this excerpt is not the point. It is simply an illustration of how one tradition can feed into the bloodstream of other traditions. In this instance an Anabaptist-Holiness tradition, a Pentecostal-Holiness tradition, and a mainline-Anglican tradition were engaged in conversation about a new paradigm never before considered by some.

I cherish the possibility of the Church of the Nazarene, the Wesleyan Church, the Free Methodist Church, the Salvation Army, and others, as churches, taking advantage of the Faith and Order opportunity to feed their own rich understandings of the apostolic faith into the bloodstream of the wider church.

6. Faith and Order is the opportunity **to develop a deeper understanding and appreciation of one's**

---

[25]O.C. Edwards in "Faith and Order Reports 1992-1995" (New York: The National Council of the Churches of Christ in the U.S.A, 1995), 21.

own tradition. It is both refreshing and challenging to explain one's tradition to those who may be learning about it for the first time. As we are pressed to explain the meaning of a particular aspect of our tradition, we are required to rethink the dynamics of it. That which within the circles of the tradition itself is dealt with in a short-hand way has to be written out in longhand, so to speak, for those unacquainted with it. The end result is that one's understanding of one's own tradition matures.

7. Faith and Order work is the opportunity for churches **to guard against becoming root bound** within their own narrower tradition. Just as root-bound plants eventually die, so do Christian traditions that limit themselves to their own little bit of Christian soil. Doctrinal development in controlled theological hot houses may lead to only superficially healthy churches. In order to be in health, all churches need to develop in the open spaces of doctrinal discussions in the church at large.

8. Faith and Order is the **opportunity for a wide spectrum of ecclesial bodies to work together** in theological endeavors. In 1982 at a Faith and Order meeting in Lima, Peru, over one hundred theologians unanimously agreed to present a statement for common study by and official responses from any and all churches willing to do so. Published under the title "Baptism, Eucharist and Ministry" (BEM), it is the product of some fifty years of study and consultation representing Orthodox, Catholic, Lutheran, Anglican, Reformed, Methodist, Disciples, Methodist, Adventist, and Pentecostal traditions. BEM has become one of the more widely discussed theological documents in the church's history.

In 1984, the Believers Church Conference (consisting of churches that stress believer's baptism) was hosted by Anderson School of Theology for the purpose of discussing the baptism section of BEM. Participants included Brethren, Mennonite, Church of God (Anderson), Adventist, Churches of Christ, Disciples, and Baptist theologians and

church historians. But also present were scholars from
infant baptism churches, including the associate director
of Faith and Order (NCCC), Brother Jeffrey Gros, a
Roman Catholic. On the basis of four days of papers and
discussion, the conference affirmed eight points of agreement with BEM on baptism, stated six points of disagreement, listed two consequences that so-called believers
churches can draw from BEM for their relationships and
dialogues with other churches, and stated four contributions that BEM can make to them as believer-baptism
churches. The report concludes by giving three sugges-
tions for the ongoing work of Faith and Order, which
included the view of some in the conference that
"Scripture. . .[should] be regarded as the sole source and
criterion of Christian belief, standing as the authoritative
corrective to our various traditions."[26]

My only reason for lifting up this last issue is not to
emphasize the "Bible only" position, but to use it as an
illustration of the opportunity that Faith and Order both
provides and promotes for a wide spectrum of ecclesial
traditions to be heard as they work together in theological
endeavors.

One of John Wesley's well-known sermons is on the
"Catholic Spirit." His text is 2 Kings 10:15, "Is thine heart
right, as my heart is with thy heart: And Jehonadab
answered, It is. If it be, give me thine hand." In the
sermon, Wesley spells out what he has in mind by one's
heart being right: it is right with God; it believes in the
Lord Jesus Christ; it is "filled with the energy of love"; it
is doing the will of God; it serves the Lord with reverence;
it is right toward one's neighbor; and it shows love by
what it does.

This "catholic spirit" is to be expressed both towards
those outside the faith and within. Regarding those
outside the faith, Wesley says that the person with a
catholic spirit "embraces with strong and cordial affection

[26]Merle Strege (ed.), *Baptism and Church: A Believers' Church Vision*
(Grand Rapids: Sagamore, 1986), 201.

neighbors and strangers, friends and enemies. This is catholic or universal love. And he that has this is of a catholic spirit. For love alone gives the title to this character: catholic love is a catholic spirit" (III.4).

Following this consideration, Wesley then deals with the catholic spirit in relation to fellow believers. He refers to love for all "whatever opinion or worship or congregation, who believe in the Lord Jesus Christ, who love God and man, who, rejoicing to please and fearing to offend God, are careful to abstain from evil and zealous of good works." Continuing, Wesley says that the one who is of a truly catholic spirit, "having an unspeakable tenderness for their persons and longing for their welfare, does not cease to commend them to God in prayer as well as to plead their cause before men; who speaks comfortably to them and labours by all his words to strengthen their hands in God. He assists them to the uttermost of his power in all things, spiritual and temporal. He is ready 'to spend and be spent for them' [cf. 2 Cor. 12:15], yea, 'to lay down his life' for their sake [Jn. 15:13]" [III.5].[27]

9. Faith and Order provides the opportunity for us to become **interpreters of other traditions at points where they may be misunderstood.** A personal example of this is Cecil Robeck's information about the traditional Pentecostal understanding regarding the distinction between tongues as the initial evidence of baptism in the Holy Spirit and the gift of tongues. Robeck, professor at Fuller and a representative of the Assemblies of God, taught all of us in that particular discussion that the classical Pentecostal position is not, as some non-Pentecostals think, that all Spirit-baptized persons have the gift of tongues. Rather, tongues speaking is simply an initial evidence of the baptism. Consequently, a person baptized in the Holy Spirit may initially speak in tongues but never again do so because they do not have the gift.

---

[27]See John Wesley, ed. Albert C. Outler (New York: Oxford University Press, 1964), 91-104.

As a result of that Faith and Order "lecture," I, as a non-Pentecostal, have been able to teach others about a Pentecostal understanding and to correct a widespread misunderstanding in my own church that Pentecostals believe that all should have the gift of tongues. Many among us point to 1 Corinthians 12:30 which asks rhetorically, "Do all speak in tongues?" and has the implied answer that not all do. Why, then, they want to know, can't Pentecostal people see the error of their ways? But that is to misunderstand the Pentecostal position. Robeck has helped me as a seminary teacher, preacher, and writer to fulfill an important role of clarifying the Pentecostal position among my own people, not so that they will become Pentecostals, but so that they will relate to others of "like precious faith" on the basis of accurate information instead of misinformation. Christian charity demands no less. In like manner, would it not be helpful to have more people in non-Holiness churches *clarifying* for those traditions Holiness terminology such as "Christian perfection" and "entire sanctification"?

Faith and Order is certainly no panacea for the dividedness of Christ's church, but it is an opportunity for that dividedness to be addressed within the context of a broad spectrum of Christian faith traditions. Many have been the times when I have been thoroughly frustrated in the meetings and by the process. There have been times when I have wondered whether it was worthwhile. But the benefits far outweigh the liabilities.

At Faith and Order meetings (twice a year), I often desire the participation of more of my Holiness colleagues in the faith. By participating, a church has much to gain. Not only may it feed into the bloodstream of the wider Christian community its own treasures of the apostolic faith, but also it can be immeasurably enriched by the treasures of the same faith which others feed into the bloodstream. But of greatest importance is this: Faith and Order is one additional small step toward the fulfillment of our Lord's prayer in John 17:21-22 that we "may all be one," to the end "that the world may believe." It is one additional feeble attempt toward responding positively to Paul's plea in Ephesians 4:1-3 for us "to lead a life worthy of the calling to which [we] . . . have been called . . . making every effort to maintain the unity of the Spirit in the bond of peace."

Appendix I

CONSENSUS STATEMENT OF FAITH[1]
by
Task Force on Doctrinal Dialogue, 1996

Preamble

We as two church movements have much with which to enrich each other. We have begun to learn from each other and must continue to benefit by building meaningful relationships. While we hold in common the lordship of Jesus Christ, we do not need to arrive at full consensus on doctrinal issues in order to be open to each other, influenced by each other, genuinely valuing and loving each other, and learning to minister with each other.

Affirmations

1. We have learned that the roles played by the Enlightenment and American Holiness/Revivalism have shaped the theological perspectives of our respective heritages.

---

[1]This statement of consensus was developed in the April 19-20, 1996, meeting in Cincinnati, Ohio, of the Task Force on Doctrinal Dialogue (names of participants appear at the end). Not in any sense meant to be a "creed," it nonetheless is an important statement of some central beliefs and observations concerning which these church leaders found themselves in full agreement after years of serious conversation with each other.

This awareness now influences our attitude and helps us to transcend certain limitations coming from our histories.

2. We appreciate the value of the historic Christian creeds, but we are unwilling to make any of these creeds a test of Christian fellowship.

3. We celebrate our common conviction that Christ is the authority for life and belief. Christ is revealed through the Bible, as interpreted by the work of the Spirit in the context of the community of faith.

4. We desire to recover for our time the essence of New Testament Christianity.

5. We recognize the church as the universal Body of Christ. Each local congregation is called to be a manifestation of this one body. We recognize the importance both of freedom in the Spirit and mutual responsibility among Christ's disciples.

6. We are agreed that baptism is commanded by the Lord Jesus to be practiced by all of His followers. This baptism is to be by the immersion in water of penitent believers. Baptism is symbolic of the atoning death, burial, and resurrection of Christ. By its nature as well as by biblical teaching, baptism is involved with forgiveness of sin. We take pains, however, to repudiate any doctrine of baptismal regeneration, holding that forgiveness is wholly a matter of God's grace.

7. We rejoice in the Lord's Supper as an affirmation of the new covenant of God's love poured out through Christ, the crucified, risen, reigning, and returning Lord.

8. We encourage our brothers and sisters in the Christian Churches/Churches of Christ and in the Church of God to give careful attention to these affirmations and to continue discussion of other issues concerning which there is a range of opinion among us. These include: footwashing as an ordinance; women in ministry; the most desirable frequency of participating in the Lord's Supper; and the meanings and processes of the "sanctification" of Christian believers.

Participants in This Statement

Christian Churches

Kenneth Cable
Byron Lambert
John Mills
James North
Lloyd Pelfrey
Richard Phillips
Bob Rae
Wayne Shaw
Henry Webb
Leonard Wymore

Church of God

Mitchell Burch
Barry Callen
Jeff Dunn
James Lewis
Vernon Maddox
Fred Shively
Gilbert Stafford
Charles Wanner

Index: Subjects and Persons